Teaching the Large College Class

Teaching the Large College Class

A Guidebook for Instructors with Multitudes

Frank Heppner

JOSSEY-BASS
A Wiley Imprint
www.josseybass.com

Published by Jossey-Bass
A Wiley Imprint
989 Market Street, San Francisco, CA 94103–1741   www.josseybass.com

Jossey-Bass books and products are available through most bookstores. To contact Jossey-Bass directly call our Customer Care Department within the U.S. at 800-956-7739, outside the U.S. at 317-572-3986, or fax 317-572-4002.

Jossey-Bass also publishes its books in a variety of electronic formats. Some content that appears in print may not be available in electronic books.

Library of Congress Cataloging-in-Publication Data

Heppner, Frank H.
  Teaching the large college class : a guidebook for instructors with multitudes / Frank Heppner. — 1st ed.
      p. cm.
  Includes index.
  ISBN-13: 978-0-470-18084-6 (pbk.)
  1. College teaching. 2. Class size. 3. Classroom management. 4. Communication in education. I. Title.
  LB2331.H47 2007
  378.1'2—dc22
                                    2007024498

Printed in the United States of America
FIRST EDITION
HB Printing 10 9 8 7 6 5 4 3 2 1

TABLE OF CONTENTS

ABOUT THE AUTHOR

Frank Heppner was born in San Francisco. He received his bachelor's degree from the University of California, Berkeley, and his Ph.D. from the University of California, Davis, followed by two years of postdoctoral work at the University of Washington. He came to the University of Rhode Island (URI) in 1969 and has had sabbaticals in the Philippines, New Mexico, and Brunei. His research specialty is organized flight in birds, and he has published papers in *Nature, Science, PNAS, BioScience,* and many specialty research and teaching journals. He has offered workshops on teaching large classes and teaching as acting at dozens of colleges internationally. He is on the honors faculty at URI, where, in addition to his large classes, he teaches a course titled Thinking and Working Like a Scientist. He served as department chair and has won a Lilly Foundation teaching fellowship and a URI president's teaching award. He is an active participant in civic affairs and is a major in the Civil Air Patrol, where he served as a volunteer search-and-rescue pilot. He is currently chairman of the Friends of Kingston Station, a historic preservation group that refurbished Kingston Station and operates a railroad museum.

PREFACE

Somehow, when we were in graduate school, the idea of teaching a huge class was something that, if we thought about it at all, was like cancer or horrible automobile accidents with body parts strewn over the highway—something that happened to somebody else. Certainly "the system" doesn't prepare people to teach large classes. At most, a few graduate schools will have a week-long training session for teaching assistants, with maybe a low-key teaching seminar, but otherwise the assumption seems to be that teaching a large class is something like sneezing: a skill that is not terribly demanding, and one that one is born with. If you know your subject, as evidenced by a brilliant dissertation in the case of a newly hired instructor, or a successful string of publications for a more senior person, what more do you need to teach a large introductory class? A great deal, as it turns out.

The "game" has changed dramatically in large colleges and universities in the past few years. In the old days, large introductory classes for majors were viewed as a kind of Darwinian filter where unsuitable students could be expeditiously screened to a manageable number at minimal expense. Large general education courses for nonmajors were a necessary evil and a sinkhole for new faculty, or those on the department chair's hit list. There were always a few thespic souls who loved big classes, but they were regarded as a benign aberration, once again demonstrating that the academy generally smiles on eccentrics.

Now, however, in large universities that were formerly funded primarily by their state governments, students' tuition payments make up an ever increasing segment of the budget, and there is increasing recognition that students pay faculty salaries. That is an attention-getting thought, if ever there was one. The old chestnut that tough professors formerly used on the first day of class—"Look to your left. Now look to your right. In four years, two of you will be gone"—takes on new meaning, when you add—"and so will your tuition payments."

With large universities engaging in aggressive recruiting competitions for students, retention of students who have been won in hard-fought (and expensive) recruiting battles assumes a new importance. If a marginal (but non-university subsidized) student can be retained for the full four years, deans and vice provosts for budget will have very large smiles. Unfortunately, the easiest way to assure retention is through grade inflation, a disease that seems to have affected even the noblest of academic institutions. In many cases this is a sure-fire (albeit questionably ethical) technique because the student has been long gone before anyone discovers that he or she can't write a coherent English sentence. However, in pre-professional undergraduate education, grade inflation is a much riskier business because most pre-professional students must take some sort of standardized knowledge test toward the end of their college careers (GRE, LSAT, MCAT, etc.), and this examination will quickly reveal that an institution's A grade is a mark of a sweet and winning personality rather than academic prowess. This information has a way of finding its way to prospective students (and their parents) to the detriment of the overly generous institution. Colleges (and professors) thus face a dilemma: How do you manage to retain increasingly marginal students without being able to use grade inflation, and without alienating the good students who reside on the other end of the curve? Even more vexing, how do you do this when many of the classes those students will take in their first two years will be enormous ones?

With present economic pressures on colleges, faculty downsizing, usually through attrition, has become the norm. At my own university, my department is half the size it was when I started more than 35 years ago, yet we have more majors and more students in our service courses than ever. This downsizing has produced two related effects: Class sizes are larger, and it is increasingly likely that professors will have at least one large to huge class a year—even those who for many years taught primarily upper division or graduate courses.

These large, typically introductory courses have assumed an importance they never before had in the economic and intellectual life of the university. Rather than being a filter, or a necessary evil, they are increasingly being viewed as the critical point of first contact with students who may or may not make it through the university, and how the course is taught may well determine whether the student becomes an alumnus or a dropout. If the class is taught well, dozens of students who enter with poor educational backgrounds, study skills, or attitudes can be "salvaged" for a full and productive four (or five) years.

But doesn't teaching a large class well take a staggering amount of faculty time? Isn't the instructor who is conscientious about teaching a big class risking his or her career, which in most large institutions is still judged by scholarly productivity? Maybe yes, maybe no—and that's where this book comes in.

Teaching large classes well is more of an art and a craft than a science. And, like any craft, it has tricks and shortcuts. But unlike a craft like cabinetmaking, one does not normally learn it through an apprenticeship. The public would not tolerate a medical system in which surgeons took coursework for four years and then were permitted to do open-heart surgery without an internship or some form of supervised apprenticeship. But in academia, we think nothing of standing someone with subject expertise, but no teaching experience, in front of a thousand students—it happens all the time. One of two things then usually occurs. The novice large-class teacher does everything he or she can possibly do to get out of the large class assignment and stick somebody else with it in a couple of years. Or, they might decide that this really isn't as bad as it seems, and it might even be fun. In which case, they begin the long process of reinventing the wheel, stumbling by themselves to discover the tricks of the trade through experience. That is how I learned how to teach large classes, and it was many years of trial and error (and thousands of frustrated students) before I began to have any real feeling that I knew what I was doing.

There are a few fine books available about teaching at the university level, but most give only lip service to the problems and practicalities of large classes. Academia has seen dozens of alternatives to the traditional large lecture come and go (e.g., audio-tutorial, personalized system of instruction, etc.), but the live lecturer in a big hall, two or three days a week, and maybe a laboratory or recitation section for the remaining credit hour remains the overwhelming structural choice for handling large numbers of students. There is today the suggestion that the web, interactive computers, and distance learning will reduce the need for large lectures. However, as Marshall McLuhan noted more than 40 years ago, video is a cool medium. Don't like what you see on the computer or television screen? Is the screen asking you to do work instead of amusing you? The flick of a finger will change it or turn it off. On the other hand, a live teacher, even in a huge lecture hall, is *in your face*. You can't turn him off or make her go away—you have to interact with a flesh-and-blood teacher. Plus, the live lecturer, even in a giant hall, can do something that computers won't be able to do for a long time—inspire students. No student ever said, "Gee, when I grow up I want to be just like Mr. Macintosh here." One can unquestionably learn some things from a computer, but as of yet it is incapable of providing a life-changing insight. Still, as Mark Twain said about the weather, everybody complains about large lectures, but nobody does anything about them.

Now, perhaps, it is time to do something about large lectures. Good teaching techniques cannot make a big class into a small class, but they can make it a much better class. The same techniques can also save an instructor a substantial amount of time.

I've been teaching large courses for 38 years. Once I reached 20,000 total students, I stopped counting. My largest single public lecture had 3,000 students, my largest class had 1,000 enrollees, and my department chair is no longer startled when she tells me that I'm going to have 300 students in Biology 101 next semester, and I reply, "Oooo—small class; they're just going to rattle around. Can't you dig up some more?" I've also been able to manage a reasonably successful research career, but not without some nimble tightrope walking. I've made every horrendous teaching error you can make, but unlike a surgeon's mistakes, mine just walk away mumbling under their breath and saying nasty things about me. Once I passed my 50th semester of introductory biology, I began to regret that my profession doesn't have a real apprenticeship for teaching—why should every young professor facing his or her first big class (or every old professor dragged kicking and screaming out of the seminar room and into the auditorium) have to make the same painful mistakes I did, and perhaps even more important, why should they not know that everybody goes through the same things and has the same problems? I couldn't think of a good reason, and that's why I decided to write this book.

Frank Heppner
University of Rhode Island
February 2007

ACKNOWLEDGMENTS

There are several people I want to thank, primarily for their inspiration. Richard Eakin at Berkeley, who died in 1999 at the age of 89, was perhaps the finest lecturer I've ever seen, and I was in awe of him when I was an undergraduate. His lectures were literally perfect—interesting, comprehensive, beautifully delivered, and acutely sensitive to the audience.

Ken Osterud at the University of Washington co-taught with me in my first large-class venture, and he showed me 47 ways students can cheat in a large class that I had never imagined possible.

At the University of Rhode Island (URI), the late Elmer Palmatier, beloved of everyone but the slacker, shared his experiences with generations of students and showed me what tough love was before the phrase was coined.

Glenn Erickson and Bette Erickson of the Instructional Development Program at URI taught me everything I know about educational theory.

My wife Marjorie was, thank God, an English major as an undergraduate, and helped with my prolixity problem and orotund prose.

Cheryl Wilga, Mike Heppner, and Jason Williams waded through the first draft of the manuscript, a task that almost defines bravery.

Carolyn Dumore guided the book through the editorial process and was a cheerful and helpful companion in what is the most stressful time in any book's life.

Finally, there are the students, bless their hearts, the thousands and thousands of students. They're the reason why we're in this business, and the reason why this book was written.

1

THINKING AHEAD

If I always appear prepared, it is because before entering on an undertaking,
I have meditated long and have foreseen what may occur. It is not genius which reveals
to me suddenly and secretly what I should do in circumstances unexpected by others;
it is thought and meditation.

—Napoleon I

Before launching forth, let me tell you the assumptions I'm going to make about you, the reader. First, I'm going to assume that you are new to teaching large classes, and possibly new to college teaching. There may be a few old futzers like me who will read this, sniff, and say, "Well, that's not how *I* do it!" but this is basically a beginner's guide. I hope that experienced teachers who browse here will recall that very little is inherently obvious the first time you do it. Second, I'm assuming that you want to do a good job and will be willing to spend some time and effort on experiments to fine-tune your course. Finally, I assume that you want to have a life outside the auditorium and will have a strong interest in tricks and techniques that result not only in a good product, but in time efficiency.

I'm also going to let you in on a little secret, one you must hide from your colleagues who do *not* teach large courses: Once the initial terror subsides, if you are a reasonably organized person, it may actually take you *less* time to teach your 400 students than it does to teach 20 in a senior-level course. It is not intuitively obvious that this is so, so when you are asked to serve on a particularly onerous committee, say Calendar and Petitions, you can roll your eyes back, shrug helplessly, and say, "I'd love to, really, but Psych 113—." This works more often than you might think, but don't try to pull it on an old hand at big classes.

There are some other advantages to teaching a megaclass. For starters, you're a celebrity. If you teach a really big course, you'll be known (for good or evil) all over the campus. At graduation time, when you are in the supermarket, young men or women, accompanied by who are obviously their parents, will discreetly point at you and whisper something to the folks, undoubtedly worshipful praise. Unlike colleagues who teach puny classes, you have a shot at getting an ovation at the end of the semester, and as a confirmed ham, I can tell you that it is a wonderful sound. But perhaps the best advantage is that if you are both conscientious and good, you *know* that you're going to have a major, dramatic, and positive influence on hundreds, if not thousands, of people. You have a marvelous bully pulpit, and as many of your students are likely to be impressionable freshmen, you can have a powerful influence for good. But before you can have that influence, you have to know what to do with that mass of humanity expectantly waiting for you to speak your first words.

First, what exactly *is* a "large" class? *Large* is a relative term, of course, but for our purposes, a large course is taught in a lecture hall with fixed seats and has a number of students greater than the number whose names you can reasonably learn by semester's end. Class sizes fit neatly in categories. Ten to 15 students is the classic small class. Discussions are easy to set up, you'll know quite a bit about each of your students, and you can be very flexible in how you structure the class. Essay exams and term papers are the norm and not burdensome to correct. Fifteen to 40 students or so doesn't represent a qualitative difference in course structure, but things are just a bit harder for you. Thirty essay examinations take a lot longer to correct than 10, for example. For me, 40–100 students is the very worst class size. You can't really teach it like a small class, and you can't justify the investment in time required to use large-class techniques. You might still give essay examinations, but you don't have time to grade them as essays— you grade using a checklist of terms and ideas you want to see.

The dividing line between "large" class and everything else is probably about 100 students. People don't expect you to use small-class techniques, and students aren't affronted if you don't know their names. On the other hand, when bullying or begging your department chair for resources, you can point out that the per-student cost for whatever it is that you want is vanishingly small. Universities that have numerical systems for figuring out faculty teaching responsibilities typically will give extra credit for teaching classes larger than 100 students due to the presumed extra workload.

Why Your Class Could Belong to the Chamber of Commerce

When you teach a large class, you need a different set of attitudes than you do when teaching a small class. A large class is *fundamentally* different than a small class in the way it has to be set up and run, and your job description is different than a small-class teacher. You are a teacher, to be sure, but you are in charge of an enterprise that is not merely a class, but something far more complex.

Your Class Is a Small Business

As the teacher of a large class, you may have up to a thousand "customers." These customers have paid a rather large sum of money for the service you provide, and some of them probably won't like it. So you need a customer complaint procedure. If you teach a laboratory course, you will have a budget, which you must request and adhere to, with dire consequences if you do not. If you have readers, graders, or laboratory assistants, you are now in the personnel business. You have to select your people, train them, evaluate them, discipline them if necessary, monitor their performance, and be able to help new hires navigate the personnel department. You are also accountable if they screw up—captain of the ship and all that. Your students will scrutinize your grading records as closely as an IRS agent might look at your tax deductions, so your accounting system has to be both accurate and powerful. There are many reasons why your customers might sue you, so you have to be aware of the legalities of grading, letters of recommendation, sexual and employee harassment, and lab safety. Students will come into your office with intense and frightening personal problems because they are away from home for the first time, and you are the only adult figure they know on campus, so you have to know when to counsel and when to refer to a professional. There can be a 50-point IQ spread in your class, and students at both ends of the spectrum expect that you will be able to teach them, so you need to know something about educational psychology. You are dealing with large numbers of people, some of whom may have very good reasons to dislike you intensely, so you need to be at least minimally aware of security. If you have a large number of teaching assistants and/or a large budget, you and your course will be of intense interest to local (campus) politicians and may either be helped or assaulted from a variety of quarters. You will be under a great deal of stress from many sources. The coach whose star forward is in your class is *exceedingly* interested in your grading policies. If students are driven away because you don't do a good job in your course, your university could lose hundreds of thousands of dollars a year. The handicapped and disabled students' office is also concerned with almost every one of your procedures, which you might at any time be asked to explain or defend. In short, you are not only a teacher, you are a *course manager.*

Once you start thinking of yourself as a course manager, not just a teacher, you can start thinking about ways to do a good job *and* save yourself some time. Some of the following phrases will help guide your thinking in this direction.

> *Sooner or later, everything that can happen, will happen, and you need to think about it and be ready for it.*

The law of averages says that if you deal with large enough numbers, even the highly improbable will eventually occur. For example, only about .05% of the American public are the unfortunate paranoid schizophrenics. Of these, about 40% have the potential for violence. That's only .02% of the total population, a tiny number. But if you have 20,000 students in your career, significant numbers of whom you flunk, you're going to have around 4 students who are unstable and may react in a potentially dangerous way when you give them bad news. Do you know how you would handle such a student in your office, if he or she became unhinged while discussing grades?

I have had students experience grand mal epileptic seizures in lecture. A woman went into labor during a final examination. A student requested an extension on an assignment because his uncle and brother were just arraigned on first-degree murder charges in a mob-related slaying, and he had to run the families' legitimate florist business for a while until things calmed down (a quite reasonable request under the circumstances, which I readily granted). A student emailed me from the state penitentiary asking what he should do about his final because he was currently being held without bail. No death threats for me (so far), but a number of bodily injury and property damage threats.

Given that you will have so many students, Monday-morning quarterbacks will say, if something goes disastrously wrong, that you *should* have thought about this particular thing, and taken preventive measures, or had a procedure to handle it. And they would be right. Remember, you're a manager, and managers are expected to foresee reasonable contingencies and take appropriate preventive or ameliorative steps. The following are some things a reasonable course manager has to think about.

Large courses can't be ad-libbed.

In a small course, if a student asks a question about a course procedure, or how she should do an assignment, you can essentially "wing it," knowing that if what you say has to be revised, it's not a big deal. In a large course, however, the minute you open your mouth, hundreds of people are copying what you say down in their notes, and they *expect* what you have to say will be authoritative and final. It is very difficult and time consuming to alter things after you've said them in a large course. Think about giving an off-the-cuff answer to a question and then regrading 750 examinations when some kid successfully argues that what you said in lecture was different than what the text said (and you had long forgotten your lecture comment). Similarly, if you are delivering a more-or-less formal lecture, most people (other than Robin Williams) have difficulty improvising in front of a huge audience, and nothing is more dreadful than standing on that stage, all eyes upon you, *knowing* that you don't have the foggiest idea what you're going to say next. This means that your degree of preparation, both in your setting up of course procedures and your actual lecture presentations, must be greater than would be the case in a small course.

A bad policy is better than an inconsistent policy.

When you are starting your large-class career, naturally you will want to do a lot of experimenting—different lecture styles, different grading systems, and so forth. However, first-year students, who are notoriously nervous about change and ambiguity, are looking for consistency in their dealings with you and your course. They have enough variables in their life without having to worry about a vacillating teacher. They know they're going to be evaluated, and they have the intuitive knowledge that if you know what's expected of you, you are more likely to meet that expectation. So they tend to react very negatively to any changes in procedure during the semester, especially procedures revolving around evaluation or assignments. Even when a change would appear to be for their benefit, say, a relaxing of the length requirement for a term paper, a lot of students will complain about it. For example, "Well, I already *wrote* ten pages, and now he only wants five. It's not fair."

Assuming you follow the suggestions in this book and think out all your procedures in advance, it is very unlikely that you will have a policy or standard so out of line that it requires a midcourse correction. If something does require some adjustment, you can usually accomplish the adjustment without publicly changing a policy. For example, let's say you're teaching a new class, and you don't really know the abilities of the students. If the first examination is a disaster and produces far fewer decent grades than you are comfortable with, you don't have to change your policy—just make the next examination easier.

The time to make changes in policy is between semesters. The only thing you will have to deal with then is the student grapevine. Large classes tend to generate stories, which develop into rumors, which in some cases become legends. Especially at a state university, there is almost always somebody whose older brother or sister took the course a couple of years back, and they will fill kid brother in on what students have to do to succeed in your course. Unfortunately, that was then, this is now, so if you do make a fairly major change in procedure between semesters, you do need to mention to students that things used to be done in a certain way but are different now. Stories on the student grapevine persist for four or five years, so you will have to repeat this warning for several semesters running. The grapevine sometimes embellishes or distorts facts. Thus, even though a story about your course might have originated years before you started teaching it, it is helpful to be aware of what's being circulated in the rumor mill so you can give students the straight story in a timely fashion.

Put it in writing.

Once you have formulated your course's procedures, assignments, and so on, commit everything to paper, and make sure your students have everything in writing. This accomplishes a number of things. First, it *forces* you to decide what your policies and procedures are going to be before the fact, rather than making such decisions on the fly. Second, it makes your life a lot easier because it takes a rich mine of excuses away from students:

> I wasn't at lecture when you announced that.

> I didn't know I was supposed to do that.

> I heard that we only needed three references.

> I thought you said Chapter 5 wasn't going to be on the examination.

> My roommate said you didn't have to type your term paper.

I give my students an extensive course outline on the first day of class (see Appendix A), and the top sheet is an affidavit that says, essentially, "I have read and understood these course regulations, and agree to comply with them. I understand there will be loss of points on assignments if I fail to follow these procedures." They have to sign and date the affidavit, and turn it in to the teaching assistant at their first recitation section. Later on, when they say they didn't know they were supposed to turn in an outline before the main paper, I can pull out the affidavit and ask them why they signed it if they didn't understand the rules.

Taking potential excuses away from students is good for them and good for you. It's good for them because if they are fully and completely informed about what they are supposed to do, they will be more likely in fact to do the correct thing. It's good for you because you have to make fewer individual decisions—there are the rules in black and white, they apply to everybody in the class, and you're just enforcing the rules, not picking on the student.

Use a checklist.

I'm a pilot, and one of the first things they tell you in flight school is *always* to use a printed checklist at critical times of the flight. No matter how many thousands of landings you've made, or how many tens of thousands of hours of flight time you have—you *always* use the checklist. The reason is that at times of high stress, if you're doing a routine job, it is very easy to skip a step and not notice it, precisely because you've done it so many times. Similarly, for the novice pilot, distractions may cause you to neglect something rather important, such as lowering your landing gear.

The same is true for a large class. Especially on the first day of class, there is a lot to do—check rosters, make announcements, and so on. The stress level is likely to be high on those first few days of class, even for old-timers. Unless you want to look like a fumbling idiot in front of a thousand people, you want to *know* exactly what things you are going to do when you walk in that class, and in what sequence you are going to do them. Appendix B shows the checklist I use on the first day of class. Even after 50 semesters of teaching the same class, I still use the checklist for the first day.

You can't save them all.

Most good, conscientious, humane teachers would like to have a positive effect on *all* of their students. This feeling is especially strong at the beginning of the semester, before some of the students have revealed themselves to be indolent sloths, or slimy, cheating sleazeballs. Nevertheless, many idealistic new teachers would like to be able to do something for everyone, especially the earnest, struggling ones, and are crushed when at the end of the semester there are large numbers of bad performances despite the teacher's best efforts. "If only I had spent more time," these teachers say. "If only my explanations were clearer, these students would have passed."

In a large class, you have a very broad representation of the human condition. Your institution may call itself a "university," but that does not mean that everyone in your class has the intellectual capacity that we used to think was necessary for a "university" education. You will probably have some students in your class who don't have a prayer of passing, because they are there to satisfy an agenda—and it may infuriate you (as it does me) when you are given students who are really nice kids but have been set up for failure by giving them "opportunities" that they have no means or readiness to exploit, at least while they're in your class.

You will also have some students who *want* to fail. Impossible, you say? Students are often strongly pushed by their parents into a particular "respectable" major. They might come from a strong, tight family, and they are not about to *defy* Mom and Dad. Not everybody who is a pharmacy major, for example, really wants to be a pharmacist.

I had a student as an advisee who had put off declaring a major, although her courses seemed to be pointing her toward pharmacy. She had been very regular in seeing me, and I had the gut impression that she was pretty smart, but you wouldn't know it from her grades. One day, when she dropped by my office, just to start the conversation going, I asked her, "So, what do you want to do when you *finish* URI?" Whoops! Wrong question. She burst into tears and wracking sobs. After she tapered off to sniffles, I asked her why the tears. Well, it seemed that what she wanted to do more than anything in the world was to be a farrier, but her dad, whom she loved beyond words, was a blue-collar guy who was determined that his daughter was going to rise above his humble status to have a profession. Pharmacy was just the ticket, and as long as he was paying tuition, that's what her major would be. A little distracted by the outburst, I thought she said that she wanted to be a *furrier,* which was really odd for a kid who had told me that she loved animals, but then it hit me that she was on the equestrian team, and she meant *farrier*—a professional horseshoer. She'd worked for one during the summer and absolutely fell in love with the job. The wheels started to turn, and I asked her if it would be okay with her dad if she became a veterinarian instead of a pharmacist. She said she supposed so, but she was pretty sure she didn't have the grades for vet school—and she was right. But I told her she could declare to be an animal science major, and she could even take courses on equine science, or whatever it is when you study horses. Her grades would almost surely pick up, and her dad would be so happy to see her in that cap and gown that he wouldn't mind when she didn't make it to vet school, and she could then take a farrier apprenticeship. Happy ending to this story—that's exactly the way it worked out, and if I owned a horse, which I don't, I would never have to pay to have it shod as long as I lived in Rhode Island—Jennifer promised me a lifetime supply of horseshoeing.

In a large class, you don't often hear about these stories, but you can be sure that there are always at least a few students out there who are going to fail no matter *what* you do, and you should not try to measure your success as a teacher by being able to get all of them safely through your course.

Start like Attila the Hun, finish as Mr. Rogers.
Everyone has a personality. Some people are affable and informal. Others are distant and reserved. However, whatever one's core personality, most people have a range of personality expressions, depending on the time, place, circumstance, and surroundings. You aren't the same person to your spouse, your kids, your friends, and the IRS auditor. Whatever your teaching personality, it will be easiest for both you and your class if you start out the semester at the most formal extreme of your personality, and then if things seem to be working out okay, you can relax a little. If you start out as a tough guy, and find after a time that the class is doing well and working hard, if you ease up a bit, the class will breathe a sigh of relief that you are now showing some human qualities. On the other hand, if you start out cozy and friendly (Don't call me Professor Farnsworth, just call me Steve), and the class gets the idea that you aren't really *serious* about things like deadlines, if you get tough later on, they will feel like you have turned against them, and aren't really as nice as you seemed to be.

Your style of dress will give the class rich clues as to the kind of personality you want to project. I always start the semester with my best suit, a power tie, and the gold pocket watch my Dad gave me. Then, as the semester wears on, if things are going well, I shift to a sport jacket, eventually lose the tie, and may even wear a sport shirt. On the other hand, if I feel they've been lazy in preparing for an exam and need a bit of talking to about this problem, back comes the suit. If I feel that they're starting to become overwhelmed and need some reassurance, I shoo the moths off my comfortable ol' cardigan sweater and do everything except change into slippers at the beginning of lecture. However, the decline of professional dress standards (or elimination of archaic dress codes, depending on your point of view) means that *formal* is now definitely a relative term. Formal in some quarters means you wear a shirt over your tee.

The personality you project will have a lot to do with the day-to-day behavior of your class. High school students are used to the idea of "testing" their teachers to find out what they can get away with in class, and then adjusting their behavior depending on the response. In recent years, they seem to be bringing that habit with them to college. Many of my colleagues are now complaining about a dramatic increase in rude behavior in freshman classes, and they are not quite sure what to do about it. I rarely seem to have this problem, and I think one of the reasons is the tone I establish on the first day of class. I try to suggest to them that they are in the intellectual equivalent of Marine recruit training, I am their drill instructor, and if they wish to find out if I really mean these things I am saying about the course, they are welcome to try me out. This approach is not for everyone, of course, but it works just fine for me. Later on in the semester, the drill instructor gets sent to the showers and is replaced by Mr. Wizard, Bill Nye the Science Guy, Beakman, or the appropriate, affable TV science teacher for your generation.

Every once in a while, however, the students get a hint that the drill instructor is waiting in the wings if they don't study, and they'd better not do anything to bring him back, because *he's out of control.* By the end of the semester, as they're getting ready for finals, I'm all tea and sympathy because the high school bravado has pretty much disappeared, and they really do need a lot of reassurance and confidence building. Going from tough to nice is appropriate given the changing needs of the students during the semester, but going the other way seems to produce student ill will at an awkward time—student evaluations of faculty.

> *Don't try to teach them as you would have liked to be taught when you were their age.*

Many conscientious new teachers make this understandable mistake. As they think about what their personal teaching style will be, they look back at those professors who had the greatest impact on them when they were undergraduates themselves. "Gee, Professor Goldschnitt changed my life—how far wrong could I go if I taught like her?" Actually, quite wrong.

If you have made it through the educational system far enough to become a college teacher, almost by definition you enjoyed school and learning. You were good at reading and eventually developed some sort of passion about your field of interest. As you went through the system, your friends and acquaintances got smarter and smarter, as those who weren't academically inclined were filtered out. You were comfortable with the life of the mind and enjoyed the challenges of using your brain.

That description may not fit all of your first-year students. What might be a terribly appealing teaching approach to a committed student might well be a turnoff or even a threat to a student who views college not as a place to learn how to use your mind, but rather as the place where you earn your union card. Colleges have abetted this view by not discouraging the aphorism, "You've got to go to college to get a good job." Does this mean that students who are in your class for the "wrong" reasons should simply be allowed to die academically while you concentrate all of your efforts on those students who are able to profit immediately from the kind of teaching approach that was so successful with you when you were a student? No. It means, rather, that you are going to have to explore a variety of teaching approaches, some of which may not be comfortable or intuitive for you, to reach those students who *can* learn, and *need* to learn, but don't learn the way the academically gifted student learns.

This is one of the reasons why it is much easier to win teaching awards if you only teach small upper-division courses than if you teach a scholastically demanding large course. In the small, advanced course, the students will be very much like you are and will respond in a similar way to your enthusiasms. In the large course, you have to study your students, find out what makes *them* tick, what rings *their* bells. The jargon term used in the education community to describe the very different ways students go about learning things is *learning styles*, and when I went through our campus's Instructional Development Program workshops on principles of learning, learning styles was perhaps the most revealing section in terms of explaining otherwise mysterious behavior. For example, most scientists involved in national panels on improving undergraduate science education argue that the old cookbook science labs don't teach students anything except rote procedures, and are boring. They advocate instead "discovery," or "inquiry" labs, which are open-ended investigative affairs that are very appealing to scientists. However, when you actually put one of these labs in place, large numbers of students stand around looking bewildered or bored, and often the most common question in the discovery lab is, "What are we supposed to do now?" Liking to perform experiments rather than replicate something that has been done before is a learning style, and designing a course around the learning style (yours) of only a few of your students invites discontent.

There are a variety of ways of categorizing learning styles, but most divide basic learning styles into contrasting pairs—for example, independent-dependent, observer-participant, and so on. It is important to note that there is not a one-to-one relationship between "intelligence" and learning style. Bright students do not all learn in the same way, and neither do average ones. In a practical sense, what this means is that in a large class, where you are likely to have *every* learning style represented, if you teach in a way that most appeals to you, you are very likely to turn off large numbers of your students.

A chemist colleague of mine had a dramatic demonstration of this when he was developing a computerized tutorial system for basic chemistry. The student would be presented with a question, and if he got it right, he would be given the next question of slightly greater difficulty. If he got it wrong, he would get the correct answer, an explanation of why his answer was wrong, and then a new question. During pilot testing, it was found that after the novelty wore off, significant numbers of students did not return for more tutoring sessions. Having a captive audience, Jim was able to ask the defectors why they weren't coming back. It turned out that many of them didn't like the *way* the tutorial worked. They didn't want the correct answer and a new question. Rather, they wanted a *hint*, then a second try. The program was revised to provide a quick diagnostic of learning style at the beginning of the tutorial session, then the presentation of the questions was appropriately modified. Participation greatly increased after the change.

What this means to you is that unless you want to appeal only to a relatively small number of students, you need to first find out something about their learning styles through questionnaires that you might obtain from your campus's faculty development office, and then mix and match both your assignments and teaching styles so that no matter what your students' learning styles are, there will at least be some tasks and teaching approaches that will appeal to them. You can't please all the people all the time.

All right, enough of the preliminaries. Let's get ready for the first day of class.

2

GETTING READY FOR THE FIRST DAY

"Where shall I begin, please your Majesty?" he asked.
"Begin at the beginning," the king said gravely, "and go on till you come to the end: then stop."

—Lewis Carroll

We're going to start at the *very* beginning of getting ready for the first day—the instant you find out you're going to teach the course. To keep the discussion focused, I'm going to make some assumptions. Let's say you are on a semester system (most common), it is the fall semester (to give you a little time to work over the summer, and because it is both more fun and more challenging to work with entering students), and you have about 250 students (about average for a large class). Further, you don't have labs or recitation sections (too complicated for right now), you have mostly first-year students, and you have some teaching experience, but not with a large class. If your course is a three-credit general introductory one, that means you will have to fill up about 39 hours worth of class time (actually 37, because you will probably have two hour-long examinations). Although there are activities other than lecture that can profitably fill that time, for the worst-case situation we'll figure that you'll have to prepare 37 or so lectures. I'll further assume that you will not have released time for preparation, and during the summer before the first class you will be teaching summer school, doing scholarly work, or wrapping up your postdoc and moving (if you are a new hire).

Several secondary assumptions fall out of the first ones. You will in all probability have other college obligations during that fall semester, for example another small course (perhaps a grad seminar), more scholarly activity, and certainly a plenitude of committees. It will therefore become increasingly difficult for you to keep one lecture ahead of your big class as the semester wears on.

So, how much time is it going to take to set up this baby over the summer? That, unfortunately, is like the question, "How much does it cost to feed a dog?"

Depends on the size of the dog.

It's the same story in preparing for a class. You can do an absolutely bare-bones job that will let you at least fill every class hour and not be too embarrassing to you and your department, or you can do the kind of job that your recruiting office can pick up on and tell prospective students' parents, "Well, yes, Jennifer here will be in Psych 113 with 450 other students, but with the magnificent, award-winning way Dr. Jones teaches it, she'll be absolutely convinced that she's the only student in the class—here, let me show you a couple of minutes of the videotape." Or, you can do what most people do: something in between. I'll show you how to figure all three ways for time budgeting.

The "Value" Course

Let's start with the minimal version. It will take you at least one hour per lecture, on average, to prepare each class session. *On average* is the key phrase, because if you fill things out with various kinds of padding and are confident enough to do some ad-libbing in areas where the topic matches your specialty, you might be able to whip out an outline in 15 minutes or so for some lecture topics. On the other hand, because this is a general course, there will be some topics that you haven't seen yourself since you were an undergraduate many years ago, and you will at least have to read the chapter in the students' textbook, and maybe look up a review article or two, so it will be a couple or three hours just for you to gain a rudimentary understanding of the topic yourself, so an hour a class is a pretty good jumping off place for the minimal version. Add a couple of extra hours of preparation for the first class of the semester. If you create a good impression on the first day, you can coast for weeks. Let's say you've spent 42 hours so far.

The syllabus and course outline will take you about four hours to think about and write out. You'll have to pick a text (if you use one), and this can eat up time dealing with publishers' reps, requesting desk copies, and so forth. Basic professionalism says you should at least skim your students' texts. Say 10 hours in text-related activities. To save time, you will use the publisher's computerized test bank that comes with the text, but these are usually dumb programs that take a while to set up, so a couple of hours there. If you are going to use anything but a multiple-choice exam, you will probably have a reader, or grader, or some such, and you will have to at least have a meeting before the semester begins—two hours. Fiddling around with a grading database will be maybe three hours (data entry is another story, but that won't take place until the semester begins). We're up to 70 hours now. Throw in another 10 hours for Murphy's Law, and you have 80 hours of preparation time for an absolutely minimal, barely professional job.

Let's say that your other professional activities in this endless summer take eight hours a day (a ridiculously low number, but nowadays, we allow for family time). If you take two weeks of time for vacation that summer, and you spend an additional two hours a day, six days a week preparing for Large Course 101, you *will* be able to get ready for it in the course of a summer—but just barely. If your department chair says that you ought to be able to get ready for a large course in less time, show him or her this book.

The "Deluxe" Course

Nobody spends the kind of time that this quality of a course requires unless it is a labor of love, and it certainly isn't a general professional expectation. Nevertheless, this is the other end of the spectrum, and you should know what's involved.

The biggest time consumer is lecture preparation. There will be more details about this in the next chapter, but the very best way to prepare a lecture is to write it out in its entirety, as a script, then either memorize it or prepare a detailed outline for reference during the lecture itself (you never, *ever* want to read aloud from a written-out lecture script). There are two reasons for writing out a complete script. First, you can get the *exact* time of the lecture so that you don't have to cut yourself off or crowd if you run long, or have to drag or fill if you run short. More importantly, you can review, in print, your exact choice of words to explain difficult concepts. It is very, very difficult to ad-lib precise explanations if you are working with sketchy lecture notes.

How many pages of script do you need for a 50-minute lecture? The rule for a screenplay is a page of script per minute on the screen. A lecture script is considerably denser, so at a comfortable speaking pace, it takes about a minute and a half to two minutes to deliver one page of double-spaced script (about 250 words). So, roughly 25–30 pages per lecture. Such a lecture will take 10–20 hours to prepare, if you're a good typist.

Clearly, nobody is going to write out almost a thousand pages of lecture notes and then memorize them for a freshman course (well, actually, some people do, but it is scarcely the norm). However, there are at least three lectures that deserve this deluxe attention, even the first time you give the course: the first lecture, which is where the students form their first impression of you; the last lecture, which is how they are going to remember you; and the lecture before you give them their student evaluations of teaching, because that's how they will rate you. So add 30–60 hours to the baseline minimal course. Other candidates for the full-bore treatment as time is available are lectures on topics that are particularly complex, where the *way* the topic is presented is critical to students' understanding.

To give the full treatment for each lecture would require a total of 400–800 hours of preparation time. If you were that ambitious, this clearly is something that you would phase in by writing a lecture or two a semester, as you gained experience in what lectures would benefit from this kind of attention.

A more typical high-quality lecture would involve 5–6 hours of research and an hour or so to make a really good outline or set of note cards. So in addition to the 30–60 hours for the three Academy Award lectures, add let's say 185 hours for the other 37 lectures.

Other extras that you would prepare for a top-drawer course that could be skipped for the minimal effort might include a procedures manual and detailed course outline for students (2–3 hours); guidelines for assignments, for example how to write a term paper (3–4 hours); problem sets when appropriate (4–15 hours); and visuals, for example PowerPoint, other media, acetate transparencies (the sky's the limit, but figure 15 minutes to an hour apiece, or 10–40 hours total). In sum, then, a really first-class job (but not one including a complete script for each lecture) would represent about 360 hours of time, or four to five times the minimal effort. The *only* way you could do that over a summer would be if you had no other professional responsibilities during that time—a compelling argument you might use with a department chair who made mouth noises about promoting and facilitating excellence in teaching.

The "Standard" Course

How much time would it take to do a perfectly respectable job, one that is clearly identifiable as more than a minimum effort, but not eat up the enormous amount of time that the full treatment requires? You can always improve lectures one at a time, as time becomes available, but first priority should go to those items that affect the course as a whole—that is, the handouts. So, 80 hours for the basics, say 60 hours for a few full-house lectures, and about 60 hours for course manuals, pre-prepared visuals, and miscellaneous distributed materials—200 hours.

All of these numbers are extremely elastic but probably represent a fair medium value for each quality level of a course. Variables include the nature of the course and topics, ease of access to reference materials, speed of typing or writing, and how much time you need (or can have) for reflection—the creative staring at the wall that laymen don't realize is often the hardest part of our job.

Background Investigation of the Course

Most large classes have a history, and none exist in a vacuum. Relatively few large courses originate de novo from their present instructors, and any introductory course that is a requirement for a major has probably existed since that major has been offered at your institution. Such courses are often prerequisites for more advanced courses, thus their content is tied to that of the higher-level courses. So, even before you start thinking about

your course outline and syllabus, it is wise to get some idea of the traditions of the course and its linkages with other parts of the curriculum.

If you can, find out if others currently on campus have taught your
course before and make arrangements to talk to them. For some strange
reason, this is often not done by new instructors, but it is a valuable source
of information. Previous instructors can give you much useful information
about problems, things that didn't seem to work, administrative hints, and
the like. Remember, however, that what you will be hearing is an *interpretation* of what the course was like, seen through the previous instructor's eyes. You will undoubtedly bring a different perspective, so it is the
information, rather than the conclusions offered by the previous instructor, that will be of greatest value to you. Talking to former students of the
course can be interesting, but information from this source must be
examined with great care because students' impressions of a course and
its instructor are strongly colored by the students' learning styles.

I had a hard lesson in how important class tradition is when I taught
my first big course at the University of Rhode Island. It was a general
education biology course that was required of *every* student in the university except biology majors. These were the days when it was thought
that there were certain things that everyone with a college degree should
know; therefore, there were university-wide required courses. Needless to
say, there were some reluctant campers in the class. My predecessor was
an elderly gentleman, let's call him Professor Todtkopf, who had been
brought out of retirement from a distinguished research career to teach
for a couple years until they found a suitable permanent teacher (there
were faculty shortages in the late 1960s). His lectures consisted of passages read aloud from the textbook, he had to be escorted to the stage in
his enfeebled condition, and he gave exactly the same examinations every
semester, confident (O! Innocence!) that because he collected the examination question sheets after each exam, there was no need to go through
the labor of preparing fresh exams each semester. Naturally, his nonvol-
untary students were delighted with his brand of pedagogy, and class
averages improved each semester, undoubtedly due to ever-increasing
study efforts by the students who were inspired by his lectures (and perhaps a well-developed fraternity exam file system).

Of course, with the arrogance of callow youth, I didn't bother to check any of this beforehand. Coming fresh from a postdoc at the highly selective University of Washington, where I had assisted in a major's course, I naturally assumed that my new students wanted a rigorous, up-to-date biology course and would be inspired by my enthusiasm. After the first examination, I had a rude awakening. The students were shocked to their very core that there were fresh examination questions that they didn't already have in their files. "Why, why, that's not *fair!*" they exclaimed. They actually got together and sent a petition to the department chair demanding that something be done about it (this was at the height of the Student Power movement). The class, the chair, and I eventually came to a *rapprochement,* but it took a couple of years to shake off the toxic dust left by Professor Todtkopf.

In evaluating the traditions of a course, perception is more important than reality. We had a wonderful example of this a couple of years back. Our Anatomy for Nurses teacher was a crusty old fellow named DeWolf. "Gruff but kindly" was probably the best way to characterize him. He had a no-nonsense approach and demanded that students actually think about the things they saw in laboratory. The student grapevine had it that he was a fierce grader, and that no one ever got an A in his course, that half the class flunked, and so on. In fact, he wasn't any tougher than any of the other instructors teaching courses at a similar level. However, at the end of the semester, when he posted his final grades you could hear the students' screams of joy from the corridor outside his office when students who were absolutely convinced that they would get a D in fact ended up with a B. It wasn't that the students weren't completely informed about their progress during the semester—the legend was that none of that mattered. The final examination was some kind of Doomsday Machine that would send even the top students back to the community college. Despite 25 years of evidence to the contrary, entering students insisted that anatomy was a killer course, and you could only pass if you had an IQ of 180. These legends and hearsays can have a strong effect on how students react to you, the new instructor, so you need to find out as much about them as possible before the course starts.

The Syllabus

I thought the word *syllabus* meant the same thing worldwide until I taught for a year in a British-style university. There, it is what our public schools call a "curriculum"—a detailed list of every fact, term, and concept to be covered during the semester—something that is rarely prepared or followed in American colleges. In American usage, it is usually just a list of lecture topics, and maybe a list of readings. I'll stick with that definition (although the dictionary's third definition of syllabus is "a list issued by Pope Pius IX in 1864 enumerating the heresies of the modern age"), and come up with another term to describe other informational documents you distribute to your students. Appendix C shows a representative syllabus.

The syllabus is really the core of your course, and you will want to spend a fair amount of time thinking about it. Get a calendar, and make a vertical column with the available class days, in this case, 39. Block out any class days that fall on a holiday. A typical number of hour examinations is two and the first thing you'll want to do is temporarily place them. If your campus has a drop date about a third of the way into the semester, as many campuses do, put your first examination about a week before it to give the students a fair chance to decide whether they want to drop. Try not to put exams immediately before or after major breaks such as Thanksgiving or spring break. Some students really do have to leave a day early because of transportation problems, and despite resolutions, a majority of students don't actually study during the break.

If you're going to have guest lecturers, try to avoid scheduling them immediately before or after an examination because some of the students' anxiety or hostility, as the case may be, will rub off on them. Similarly, find out when you will be administering student evaluations of teaching, and avoid exams around that period. This will now leave you with about 35 classes to fill.

If you will be using a textbook (as many introductory classes do), unless your classes pretty much follow in synch with the book reading assignments there will be a surprising amount of student resistance. Students really seem to like you to lecture on topics that they are currently reading about. Thus, if you're reasonably happy with the sequence of topics in the book, it's not a bad idea to sequence your lectures in the same order as the book. If you're not entirely happy with the order in the book, there will be fewer problems if you scramble the order of the chapter reading assignments, then have your lectures pretty much follow the new order.

It will rarely be the case that you will want to spend the same amount of time on a given topic that the text author does. Maybe you will want to spend more time on your specialty, for example. That's okay—students seem to accept that idea if you tell them that you're not always going to be in *exact* synch with the book during your first lecture. However, if you spend proportionately more time on one topic than the book does, try to spend a little less time on the next one so you don't get further and further out of phase with the text.

Once you have the general sequence of topics in mind, a convenient next step in preparing the syllabus is to block out the semester into sections, perhaps 10 or so, each of which logically flows into the other. In my general biology course, for example, I have sections on ecology, kinds of animals, genetics, and so forth. These sections might in turn be divided into three hour-long lecture classes. Now is the time to start thinking of individual lecture titles. It is also the time to schedule "orphan" lectures—single lectures that are important but don't really fall into one of your sections. For example, in my general biology course, I have orphan lectures on the biological basis of myth and legend, the history of biology, and Western and non-Western theories of health and disease. These don't really fit in any of the sections, but they're kind of fun, with lots of pictures, so I slip them between sections that are, shall we say, of a more rigorous nature.

Now you have the first approximation of your syllabus. You would then fine-tune it with the following considerations. The day before holidays, large numbers of your class will be gone, many unavoidably, so you might not want to schedule a critical topic on that day. Deplorably, Friday morning attendance at many campuses is frequently lower by 30% than on other days. You can address it three ways: by ignoring it, by resigning yourself to it and avoiding critical lectures on Fridays, or scheduling quizzes or assignment turn-ins on Fridays. I have found it almost completely ineffective to tell students that information from Friday lectures most definitely and positively will be on examinations—even after the first examination reveals this to be true. Whatever it is they do on Thursday nights that keeps them from Friday lectures is clearly more important to them than the hypothetical loss of a few points. I find that Friday attendance is down even with premed students, something that was unheard of even five years ago. Sign of the times.

Once you have pretty much locked in the dates and topics of the lectures, and provided dates for the examinations, you can fill in the other items customarily included on a syllabus: reading assignments and chapter/lecture responsibilities for examinations. How much reading a week is reasonable for students? It depends on what you mean by "reasonable," and the average reading ability of your class. This is really a question that can only be answered with a couple of years' experience with a particular class, but I would suggest that in the first semester that you teach a new class, you schedule the *minimum* amount of reading you feel comfortable with. You don't want to *unnecessarily* develop a reputation as an unreasonable ogre who doesn't know students have other classes. You might have taken a similar course when you were an undergraduate. How much reading was there? Remember, you were probably an excellent student, so if your recollection was that the reading load was very reasonable to easy, then that might be just about right for your new course. If your recollection was that it was too much, then almost certainly it will be too much for most of your students. This recollection needs to be tempered with the realization that you might be teaching to a different clientele than you were part of when you were a student. I can tell you that *my* biology majors can grudgingly handle about 100 pages of technical text a week, but that doesn't really do you any good. Your present colleagues are probably the best source of information on reasonable reading expectations for your students.

The final item that appears on almost all syllabi is a list of the reading and lecture assignments for turned-in work, quizzes, and examinations. This information must be as specific and detailed as possible. On the syllabus, I usually say something like this: "For the first examination, students are responsible for the material in all lectures through 24 February, and Chapters 1, 3, 5, 7, 8, and 9 in Ginsburg. For the second examination, students are responsible for all material required for the first examination, plus lectures through 7 April and Chapters . . ." Coming from high school, most students *expect* that examinations are not cumulative—that is, the first examination covers the first third of the book, the second examination covers the second third, and the final covers the last third, with perhaps a few questions from earlier chapters. Thus, you must be very explicit about your requirements, particularly if they differ from this expectation.

The Course Manual

The course manual contains all the other information students will need to satisfy your requirements and do business with your course. It is usually handed out with the syllabus, or the syllabus is the first section of the manual itself. Appendix A shows the course manual in my large course.

There is disagreement among experienced teachers over how comprehensive the course manual should be. Some argue that the longer it is, the less likely some students are to read any of it. I agree with that view, but I think that is an acceptable price for making sure that the conscientious student has all the information he or she needs. One thing is sure: If you *tell* students critical course information in the first lecture and depend on them to include it in their notes—good luck. If you tell them *and* give them a handout, there will be a fair chance that some of it will sink in.

What should be included? At a minimum, housekeeping information (location of your office, office hours, phone number, etc.), deadlines for turned-in work, makeup procedures (if any), basic outline of your grading system (very important), and statements of policy on late work, cheating, plagiarism, and the like.

Selecting and Ordering Texts

Many large classes use textbooks, and the textbook publishing business has changed dramatically in the last 20 years with both the consolidation of publishing companies and the fierce competition that exists among the survivors. The result of these market forces is that there are very few bad texts on the market today, but for a given field, most of the offerings are very similar.

If you teach in a field that traditionally uses texts and you now find yourself teaching a large course, you will find yourself the subject of attention by traveling representatives of the publishers. These folks *really want* to be of assistance to you because if you adopt their book, the publisher may be looking at $50,000 in revenue from your one adoption. You normally don't have to worry about finding them—they will find you.

There are a few ethical guidelines in dealing with publishers' reps. Cash kickbacks to professors have never been the custom, nor are they okay. Personal presents to you are not cricket, but sometimes for a large adoption a rep will throw in a piece of equipment to your department, if you don't have, for example, a DVD player that you can use with course materials. If a rep takes you out to lunch, most campuses don't consider it a breach of ethics.

The rep will give you a free examination copy of their book for you to evaluate, and if you adopt the book, will give you a reasonable number of free copies for your assistants. Many texts come with an "adoption package" that includes an instructor's guide, computerized test bank, and audiovisual materials (including transparencies, PowerPoint discs, etc.). There can be some differences between these packages, and it is worthwhile to ask the rep for a sample.

With the advent of the used-book marketplace, textbooks are revised nowadays on a two- to three-year cycle, whether they really need it or not. The old edition often becomes very difficult to obtain once the new one comes out, so you are almost forced to adopt the current edition. This can be an inconvenience because the topics in chapters often change subtly, and you then have to write up a new syllabus.

If you are fortunate enough to teach your class by yourself, you pick your own textbook, and that's the end of it. If your course is committee taught (as many introductory courses are), there will be a committee text choice, and you should prepare yourself for endless wrangling when this committee meets.

I always form a small panel of students to look over texts when I have to select a new one. Students, after all, are the ones who have to study from the book, and I have received some valuable insights from students as I consider a new book.

Course Budgets and Ordering

A course that consumes things, such as laboratory supplies, obviously needs a budget. Even a straight lecture course needs a budget. A one-page handout for 300 students costs *somebody* 15 bucks. Sometimes the course budget is invisible to you—your handouts, office supplies, and so forth are included in the office budget. Most of the time in that situation, you can blithely distribute handouts to your heart's content, but really big courses can start running up significant and conspicuous printing bills if you are too enthusiastic, and in hard budgetary times you might find yourself with a quota on materials to be distributed. If you are under pressure to cut down on handouts for budgetary reasons, a few layout tricks can dramatically reduce your reproduction bills. Nothing says that a handout has to be beautiful, so you can go to quarter-inch (instead of inch) margins all the way around except the left side, so students can bind the handouts. Going to 10 point type like this can let you get a lot more on the paper, and it is still fairly readable. Going to seven point type is probably stretching it, though. Naturally, you will print on both sides if you have a modern copier.

If you are teaching a course for the first time, ask whoever keeps the books in your office to let you see the budget history of your course for the past five years. While you're at it, ask to take a look at the budgets of other large courses that are roughly comparable in gross expenses. Plot a few of them against your course. This will give you some idea whether your course has historically gotten its fair share of the budget.

Most departments operate on a fiscal year basis, and typically that year begins July 1. What that means in practical terms is that usually the department runs out of money about April or so in the following year. Thus, if you find out in May that you will be teaching a laboratory course in September, and like a good citizen you submit your supplies order in June, the order probably won't even leave your campus until July or August, and you will be lucky if you get your first shipment by mid-September. Thus, while planning any activity, such as a lab, that uses consumables, it is prudent to check well in advance to see if you have enough supplies on hand to carry you for a month or two into the new semester until your orders start coming in. If you are lucky, your predecessor will have done this for you. So, one of the very first things to do when you find out that you will be teaching a supplies-intensive course is to do an inventory of items that traditionally have been used in the course. If you find that the supplies are thin, prudence would then say to shuffle the activity requiring consumables to later in the semester to give yourself a chance of getting an order completed before the scheduled activity. This is pedagogically terrible because things can get out of synch between lecture and laboratory, but is a regrettable fact of life of college budgeting.

Another distressing budgetary unpleasantry is something called a "rescission." I didn't even know what one was until about five years ago, when I was "recissed." In a rescission, before the next fiscal year, the department chair tells you that you can spend, say, $2,000 on your course. Then, halfway through the semester, the head finds out that the dean has reclaimed half the department's budget due to some real or imagined campus emergency. All of your orders in the pipeline are then frozen, and you are left with the intriguing creative challenge of figuring out how to do a Dissection of the Rat laboratory without rats.

The natural response on a campus where there have been rescissions is the appropriately paranoid one—you spend your entire course budget in the first week of the course, so the dean will get nothing when he or she later sucks up the balance of your budget. Naturally, this is a terrible way to do business; you can't respond to changing enrollments, you have to engage in a variety of ingenious lies to get suppliers to deliver market-price perishables eight months after they're ordered, and you have no cushion left for emergencies. I don't, therefore, recommend the order-everything-at-once scheme unless there have been rescissions before, or the grapevine hints that your campus might be a candidate for a foreclosure sale.

A good habit to develop if you will be teaching the same supplies-intensive course for several semesters is that followed by the industrious woodpecker. They know that although there are many acorns now, there will be none this winter, and next summer might be slim pickin's. So they hoard. A very good idea for academics. Any nonperishable item that can be inconspicuously stashed away, such as test tubes, should be ordered in slight excess for a couple of years, until you have a decent emergency supply. The operational word is *slight*. This is a survival/emergency strategy, but not one that is welcome by the people in the budget office who created the situation that forces you to use it, so you will want to be as inconspicuous as possible.

Handouts

My general biology class is rather demanding and uses a huge textbook. I know my students are intimidated by the 1,100 pages of fact-packed text, and I always used to reassure them by saying, "Look, I know the text is big, but it's a reference book as well as a textbook, and I'm only going to hold you responsible for the *important* concepts." My conscience thus clear, I blithely assumed that they would ignore the picky detail stuff and concentrate on the broad ideas that I had in mind when I said "important concepts." This confidence was rapidly dissipated when I noted that on examinations they did pretty well on the occasional picky detail question, and totally bombed out on the broad conceptual questions. So I decided to try an experiment.

I copied the summary page from a chapter they had just read about the kidneys and the excretory system. It consisted of 14 numbered paragraphs. I distributed the copies to them in lecture class. I then asked them to write down for me the five *most* important ideas on that sheet—ideas that were so important that they would remember them 10 years from now. I then told them that to show them what a nice guy I was, I'd give them an example of such a major concept: "The kidney has something to do with regulating the balance of salt and water in the body." However, from the way they were gnawing on their pens I could tell they were having difficulties. I gave them a couple of minutes, then pointed to a student and said, "Okay, give me an important concept."

"The-proximal-convoluted-tubule-is-longer-than-the-distal-convoluted-tubule."

What?! This was about as picky as you could get. A series of similar answers told me that *their* idea of an important concept was very different than *my* idea. So, after class, I dropped by the labs to talk to several of them individually, and found that to a typical student "important concept" means "a phrase or expression consisting of a large number of huge words whose significance or meaning is totally beyond my grasp." So, by telling them to concentrate on something that was very different from my understanding, I was in effect driving them into behavior that was exactly the opposite of my intention.

Now I make it absolutely explicit what I want them to be *responsible* for in their studies. First, in the course outline handout they get on the first day (see Appendix A), I tell them specifically what responsible means. Then, they get a series of handouts during the semester that tell them exactly what terms and ideas I, as a professional, think are most important.

Some of my colleagues have chastised me for doing this. "Spoon-feeding," they sniff. And truth be told, I have some reservations myself—it is an important skill to be able to identify key ideas buried in trivia. However, many of my students have been spoon-fed for 12 years, and I feel that it is unreasonable to ask them to give up the spoon cold turkey. Also, the thing that enables a professional to decide what to read among the mountains of information that crosses a desk every day is experience, and by definition, first-year students don't have much experience. Nor do many of them yet have college reading ability. So, they get these lists for every chapter in the first third of the course, every other chapter in the second third, and not at all in the final third.

Other handouts many instructors distribute to large classes include problem sets where appropriate, guidelines for term papers, brief guides to library use, using the Internet, lab instructions, and so on. I always have about 25% more handouts printed up than the class size to take care of the inevitable dog eating the handout, and following the assumption that it is the student who most needs the handout who is least likely to read it, I generally discuss the handout, even at the cost of more productive lecture time, during class. If your school has the capacity to put handout material online, you can cut down on the number of requests for lost handouts.

Checking Out the Physical Facilities

Every lecture hall is different and will require differences in your presentation technique, so it is generally a good idea to check out your "theater" very early in your preparation process. How big an image can the projectors produce? (It makes a difference when you prepare transparencies or PowerPoints.) How are the acoustics? (This determines whether you'll need a mike.) If you use a blackboard, is there enough light on it to see writing from the back of the room? (Probably not—the people who design academic auditoriums often seem to have gotten their architecture degree from MeriLee's College of Beauty and Lecture Hall Design.) I'll give you more details in the next chapter, but the layout of the auditorium will have a lot to do with the audiovisual materials you make and the lecture techniques you can use.

Reading Assignments and Lectures

How much reading/homework is reasonable to assign to your students? It's a tough question—*reasonable* is a relative term. You need to make a decision about this before you draw up your syllabus because reading assignments should be included on it. I can't really make a specific recommendation to you because so much will depend on your course, your college's traditions, and the quality of your students, but I can give you some guidelines.

I can say without fear of serious dispute that high school students today do not do as much homework as they did a generation ago. My recent first-year students—science majors at a main-campus state university—averaged 45 minutes a night's worth of homework *total* in all of their subjects when they were high school seniors. A quarter of them had no homework at all—study hall was sufficient. Therefore, when I tell them that they can expect to work two hours a week outside of class for every credit hour, or in my case, eight hours a week, or an hour and a half or so a night *on my course alone*, the reaction ranges from incredulity to stunned disbelief to "yeah, right." In checking around the campus, if there is such a thing as a "standard" for reasonableness in reading/homework assignments, it does seem to be two hours of outside preparation (reading) for every credit hour for a demanding course. Inquire around your campus and see what other people are assigning in your general type of course (major, nonmajor, first-year, etc.), and if you are not far off the average, you won't have to deal with howling mobs of students bearing spears and torches outside your office.

So let's say you want to keep them busy for 8 to 10 hours a week. What does that translate into as a reading assignment? Well, hopefully the good students will be doing more than just reading. They'll be outlining, writing notes, reviewing, answering questions, and so on. So, figure half to a third of their total homework time should be allocated to activities, rather than just reading. That leaves four hours for reading. How much can students read (and absorb) in four hours? A simple experiment will tell you. Grab their textbook (or whatever you are having them read), and read a "unit," say a chapter, yourself. See how long it takes you to read it. Now take that number and add 50% to it, because 1) the students will be unfamiliar with the material, and 2) they are probably not as fast a reader as you are. So if it takes you an hour to read the chapter slowly and carefully, it will take your students an hour and a half. Two and a half chapters a week would be reasonable, then. You can always *assign* them more reading than your experiment would suggest, but it is likely to be counterproductive because the students will become frustrated first, then resentful.

A fact of today's student life that has to be incorporated into homework assignments is the ever-present bugaboo of part-time jobs. For some students, the part-time job may be a matter of survival, but I also hear this lament all the time from my middle-class students—they can't do the homework because they have such long hours at their jobs. It is certainly true that many students at public colleges and universities have part-time jobs, in many cases 20 hours a week or more, and, to be sure, there are many students who really need to work those hours to stay in school. But I am increasingly finding that my students, who at my institution are generally lower- to upper-middle class, are not working because they need every penny for tuition and books, but to support a lifestyle they got used to in high school when their parents were subsidizing them.

Every semester, I ask my students how many of them have part-time jobs. Almost all. How many of them live on campus? About half. Those who live on campus, how many have cars? About half. How many of them have MP3 players? Almost all. How many have paid more than $75 for athletic shoes? Almost all. It seems to be very hard for many students who are used to this kind of living to give it up, even temporarily. I had an advisee, a pre-vet, very bright, who started out doing well in her first year, but then things started falling apart rapidly. When I asked her about it, she said she was working 30 hours a week, and she just didn't have enough time for study. Why so many hours? Skiing. She *loved* to ski, and every weekend in winter she was on those expensive slopes with the $500 Rossignols. I told her that if she wanted to be a vet, she'd have to cut out at least half of her work hours. Well, no, she couldn't really do that, but she'd just study harder and more efficiently. There was a happy ending (sort of) to the story. She eventually *schussed* her way out of the University of Rhode Island and into a job as a ski instructor/bum in Colorado, which is, I suppose, what she really wanted to do in the first place.

Relatively new to the medium to large universities that typically have large classes are significant numbers of older than average or returning students. This clientele has long been a fixture at community colleges. Many of these students have families, jobs, and a very real time-budgeting problem. I have found that over the years this group does just about as well, on average, as traditional-age students. Whereas they might have more time constraints, they also tend to be more focused and disciplined than younger students. When I have some older students in class, I always give them a few words of encouragement at the first lecture. I tell them that the only student who ever got a perfect score in my class was a 30-year-old paraplegic woman. They seem to be heartened by this true story.

Disabled Student Matters

In recent years, campuses have made a great effort to comply with the provisions of the Americans with Disabilities Act by extending what is legally defined as "reasonable accommodation" to students with disabilities, including learning disabilities.

Before you start your large class for the first time, you should have a chat with your campus's disabled students' office to review what policies they have that might affect your teaching. On my campus, only students who have been "certified" by the disabled students' office are eligible for accommodations, and they must provide an instructor with documentation to that effect at the beginning of the semester.

I have not had any real problems complying with any requests for accommodation I've received so far. Allowing a student to tape a lecture or use a notetaker presents no difficulty, nor does allowing a student extra time on an examination. The only accommodation I sometimes have difficulty with is allowing the student to take an exam in a private, quiet room. I am usually shorthanded with exam proctors to start with, and detaching one to supervise the lone student in a room is sometimes difficult to manage.

Deciding on a Grading Plan

I'll give you some suggestions on setting up your testing and grading system in Chapters 7 and 8 (assessment and grading), but settling on some kind of grading scheme is essential before the semester begins. Students are as sensitive about their grades as you probably are about your paycheck, and they hate change and uncertainty. Your grading system is not something you can jigger with during the semester if you don't like how it is working, so it is worth whatever amount of time is necessary to think about and spell out your grading plan in advance so you can include it on a handout at the beginning of the semester.

Assembling a Lecture

There are some general guidelines for any lecture.

1. Every lecture should have a beginning, a middle, and an end. The lecture should follow the rule, "Tell them what you're going to say, say it, and tell them what you've said." Note that a lecture can be longer than a single class period, but if it must be broken up over several periods, at the end of each one there should be a "running summary" that sums up the day's talk, and a fairly extensive recapitulation at the beginning of the next period.

2. Attention span limitations make it a good idea to break the lecture every 15–20 minutes with a 1- to 5-minute activity. This can be a simple "What are the three most important things you've heard in the last 15 minutes?" or a mini-discussion of some question you have thrown out.

3. Because of listener fatigue, introduce your most complex ideas at the beginning of the period. After 40 minutes of even the most brilliant exposition, ideas tend to run into one another in the listener's head. When it's feasible, complicated ideas should be introduced as early as possible in the lecture, then developed fully before moving on. If you present a complex new idea toward the end of the period, you won't have time to explore it properly, and for all practical purposes you'll have to present it from scratch in the next period.

4. It takes at least 15–20 minutes to present a genuinely new idea. It takes quite a while to present the idea, give a couple of examples, try to connect it in some way to something they already know, give another example or two, present it from a different viewpoint, and summarize. At most you can only present about three brand-new ideas per period, if you want to have any hope that they will actually understand what you said. You can *present* a lot more new ideas than this during one period, but most of the students will simply be overloaded transcribers.

In presenting new ideas, the notion of constructive redundancy is helpful. Simply to repeat what you just said several times is boring. Instead, try to come up with a couple of different perspectives, and present them as, "Let's now look at it this way."

What it really comes down to is that a lecture is a lousy way of transmitting facts to people—reading or the web are much more efficient at that job. Where a lecture is unsurpassed is in explanation of complex subjects, motivation, and tying apparently disparate subjects together. Appendix D will show you a sample of a complete lecture.

The First Day of Class

After all of the hours of thinking and preparation, your first day in front of a big class will eventually come. And if you're like 90% of all the first-time big-classers I've seen, you'll be nervous as hell. That's good. That's normal. Stage fright, if controlled, gives you the kind of energetic edge you'll need to engage your students. So how do you keep it within bounds?

For starters, there's good preparation. You don't want to walk into the class in a panic because the office hasn't finished copying your syllabus. Everything that you will bring into the class should be assembled in a staging area a day or so before, and checked out. You will have looked over your own handouts in detail, so if students ask you questions about grading, you'll be able to answer them without hesitation. If you will be using the Internet as part of your instruction, you will already have established the proper accounts and set things up (Chapter 5). You will have checked with the bookstore weeks in advance to be sure that the texts are in and sufficient in number for your enrollment. It normally takes two to three weeks to fix a book order error, so this is something that cannot wait until the last minute. You will be familiar with your campus's registration system, so if students need to get into or out of the course, or change recitation sections, you'll know what to say. You will have made nice to the audiovisual or instructional technology people so there will be some reasonably competent person present or available in case the PA starts acting weird. You will have an extra battery for your wireless mike, if you use one, and know how to replace it. Ditto for a bulb for the overhead projector. You will know what do when Windows crashes, and will have a backup plan if the last person who was using the auditorium pushed all the wrong buttons on the computer projector. Just in case the instructor who precedes you in the auditorium has walked off with the mike just before your lecture, you will have previously practiced a bare-voice presentation in the auditorium, and the fact that you are mikeless will not be noticed by the students.

Confident in your preparations, resolved to be flexible in the face of any little irregularities (such as a student standing up and shouting obscenities as you begin—no problem, just a case of Tourette's syndrome), you have only one task remaining before taking the stage. You have to decide who you are. The next chapter will help you make that decision.

3

THE TEACHER AS ACTOR

There's no business like show business.

—Irving Berlin

What are the technical differences between you, facing your class of 400 in Soc 101, and Sir John Gielgud, contemplating the skull of Yorrick as he performed *Hamlet* at the Old Vic in London? None. Both of you are working in front of an audience, whose seats are bolted to the floor facing the stage. Members of that audience have paid substantial sums of money to be there. You are in a theater. The person sitting in the back of the theater has a reasonable expectation of seeing and hearing pretty much what the person in the front row does. Information flow is primarily from the stage to the audience. And unless that audience connects somehow with the person on the stage and the information being delivered, the results will be identical. The audience will pass into slumber.

You are an actor when you teach a class, in the sense that you have the same delivery problems that the stage actor does. You both need to be seen, heard, and understood. You need to convince each member of the audience that you are connecting to him or her, personally. The skills that a stage actor uses to deal with these issues can be adopted almost without modification to the large class context. Using an actor's skills in a large class does not mean being hammy or histrionic. It simply means that to reach a student who is sitting perhaps 50–75 feet away from you in an auditorium, and have that student forget that he or she has hundreds of classmates, involves some public speaking/acting skills that are too often neglected by large-class teachers.

An actor needs to know five things: his character, his lines, his stage-craft, his theater, and most importantly, his audience. We'll look at each of these things in turn.

Character

You might be saying to yourself, "What is this guy talking about, 'character'? I'm me, who else?" Well, yes, but are you the same person to your spouse, your parents, your friends, your colleagues, and your children? Everyone appears different to different audiences, and you have a wide latitude in indicating to your students who "you" are.

Consider teachers in the movies. John Houseman in *The Paper Chase*—brilliant, austere, challenging, aloof. Edward James Olmos in *Stand and Deliver*—compassionate, dedicated, challenging, caring. Michelle Pfeiffer in *Dangerous Minds*—tough, involved, challenging. Everybody seems to like to give a challenge. Robin Williams in *Dead Poets Society*—creative, wildly imaginative, dumb. Dumb? He got fired in the end—hard to inspire young minds in the unemployment line.

All of these disparate personality types made for effective teachers—at least in the movies. How would *you* like your students to see you? Captain of the vessel *USS Pedagogia*? The boss? A friend? A guide? A coach? An elder statesman? By your dress, your manner, your mode of speech, your position onstage, you can define your character for your students. Whatever you decide you want your stage persona to be, it is important that you feel comfortable and natural in that role.

I had this lesson rubbed in my face the first time I gave a lecture on human sex anatomy to a thousand students, back in the 1960s. When I was a grad student, a wonderful embryology professor at University of California, Davis, Milton Hildebrand was famed far and wide for giving the *details* about human sexuality in his junior-level embryology course. The real stuff, including contraception, which at the time was still a bit of a taboo. When he came to this block of lectures, they moved his class to the largest lecture hall on campus because so many outside students wanted to sit in. This was at a time when accurate sex information was impossible for high school students to get, and difficult for college students (my, how times have changed!).

Hildebrand was in his 50s, and he talked about even the most sensitive subjects in a kindly, almost grandfatherly way. All of the biology grad students in my cohort were in awe of his ability to use words like *penis* and *vagina* in front of a general audience without embarrassment, and I resolved that when I got my own biology class, I, too, would provide this great service to my students.

When it came time for me to give this difficult lecture, the problem was that I was 29, didn't look much like a grandfather in my tie-dyes, and worst of all, I wasn't a naturally serious sort of person. When I tried to emulate Hildebrand's kindly elder manner, almost like a Mr. Rogers for college students, as soon as I got to the nitty-gritty I started to lose it. As I started in on Mechanism of Erection, the first snickers appeared. I knew that under no circumstance should I crack a joke, leer, or indicate in any way that the subject was less serious than the death penalty or genocide, but I couldn't help myself. No amount of thinking about the Giants' terrible record helped. As if I were listening out-of-body, I heard myself say, "If you want to get an erection, you have to start with an Erector Set." An Erector Set was a very popular children's construction toy in the 1950s made out of steel that you could use to build towers, skyscrapers, and other phallic monuments. The class sat stunned for about five seconds—they had been trying just as hard as I was to be serious and adult about all this. Then they lost it, too. Gales of laughter billowed out, and it was five minutes before I could begin to restore order. Afterward, I realized that "doing" a kindly, senior professor was outside both my natural personality and my acting skills at the time. Regretfully, I now find that I can easily play a kindly, old professor.

So what can you use to shape your character? Costume, for starters. Students will form a difficult-to-change impression of you in the first few seconds you appear onstage, so you want to devote some thought to what you will wear on that first day. Following the start-as-Atilla-the-Hun-end-as-Mr.-Rogers principle elucidated in the first chapter, whatever is the formal end of dress you are comfortable with is the place to start. You will be perceived as more or less of an authority figure depending on your choice of wardrobe. If it is important for your students to follow rules and procedures, a suit and neckwear will help them understand you mean business. On the other hand, that degree of formality will get in the way if you want to develop a relaxed atmosphere right from the beginning.

There is no rule that says your character's dress has to be consistent during the semester. If you need to ream them out, the power suit reinforces your words. If they are discouraged and need a boost, something warm and fuzzy will be reassuring. The only real rule is that you be comfortable and natural wearing whatever you do.

Where you stand onstage will shape students' impression of you. If there is a lectern, your relationship to it will exert a powerful effect on students. A lectern is a symbol of authority. If you stand behind it, hands invisible, notes in front of you, you are in full Lecture Mode, with the majesty and power of a thousand years of academia backing you up. There can be no doubt about who's boss in *this* course. If you are naturally shy, diffident, or uncertain of yourself because you've never done this, the lectern can give you some impressive backup. On the other hand, it is hard to convince the students that you are a regular sort of person and have their interests in mind if you never leave the security of the lectern.

If, on the other hand, you stand in *front* of the lectern, that demonstrates a real (or well-acted) confidence. You don't need the shield of the lectern to protect you from your students. Standing by the side of the lectern, with one hand casually resting on it, will also present a picture of easy confidence and mastery of the situation.

Lines

An actor's lines come from his script. Your lines come from the text of your lecture. The text of *Hamlet* is always the same. However, our impressions of the character Hamlet differ enormously depending on the actor's rendering of the role. Similarly, how you deliver your lines can make a big difference in how students interpret your text.

There are several ways you can deliver your lines: 1) Write out a word-for-word script, then read from it. 2) As above, but memorize it. 3) As above, but make an outline or cards from it. 4) Start with an outline or cards that you bring to class, and ad-lib the details. 5) Ad-lib the whole shebang.

I would respectfully discourage the first and the last. Reading from a script is absolutely deadly from an audience perspective. There is no eye contact, no body language—they might as well be listening to a tape recorder. Ad-libbing is a rare gift, and to be able to ad-lib an entire lecture, especially one on a technical subject, is not something I can show you how to do.

There are real advantages to writing out a lecture in its entirety. You can get the timing right, so you end where you want to. Unless . . . you . . . are . . . a . . . real . . . slow talker it will take about two minutes a page to deliver. You can also get the wording of difficult explanations exactly right. Once you have your script, you can extract the "meat" and put it in outline or card form. A lot of people use cards, and they have the advantage of being easily edited, but if you drop them during a lecture . . . A page outline has the advantage of forcing *you* to organize what you have to say in outline format, and that is exactly the note-taking format that beginning students find most beneficial.

Stagecraft

An actor has three major tools: voice, hands, and body. Let's talk about voice first.

Voice
There are three simple rules to follow:

1. You have to speak so they can hear you.

2. You have to speak so they can understand you.

3. You can't put them to sleep.

To find out how you're doing you need to have 1) an audio recorder, and 2) a really good friend, one who will be honest with you.

You cannot, by yourself, assess how audible you are in an auditorium without a lot of experience. The easiest way to check this out until you get that experience is to have Trusted Friend sit in the back of your class, when the class is in session, and see if she can hear you. You might try using a mike and going mikeless. As there are often acoustic dead spots in poorly designed auditoria, several locations should be tried. If you can be heard easily without the microphone, and your voice doesn't sound strained, then you're ready for the next step. Otherwise, it's time to learn how to use a microphone.

There are only two mike types in general use in academia: the hand-held and the clip-on, also called a lavalier. Nowadays, they both tend to be wireless or radio operated. I sort of miss the old mike cord. You could do some great gestures by whipping the cord around. Nevertheless, the cordless mikes reduce the possibility of making yourself a total idiot onstage by getting tangled in your mike cord. However, because the wireless mikes are really little radio transmitters, they still require power, in most cases a nine-volt battery. Always carry a spare, and know how to change it—dead batteries are the most frequent cause of microphone malfunction, especially in the first class of the day, after forgetful colleagues have left the power switch on all night.

The handheld mikes are generally of superior audio quality and give your voice a great deal of flexibility. You can whisper into one, or move it to one side while you cough, sneeze, or belch. You can also use it as a pointer. The disadvantage, and it is a large one for many people, is that it ties up one hand, making it more difficult to write using an overhead projector.

Unfortunately, despite its many advantages, it is easily possible to misuse a handheld. They are designed so that the business end should be no more than an inch or so away from your mouth. If you are not consciously aware of keeping it there, what often happens is that as your arm tires, the mike starts to drop toward your navel. You cannot easily hear the difference, so by the end of the lecture your voice has completely disappeared from the rear of the auditorium. Another frequent problem is that speakers will hold the mike rigid in space as they look to left, center, and right of the class. As a result your voice sounds like this on the left, then gets real loud in the center, then shrinks down as you face right. The easiest way to handle this is to keep your upper arm tucked into your side, then imagine that the head of the mike is glued to your mouth—whichever way you face, the mike head goes with you. Watch a television newscaster or singer to see how it's done.

The lavalier was designed to be idiot-proof, but alas, there is no such thing. The little clip-on mike head is designed to be used as high up on your chest as you can get it, preferably at throat level. If you clip it closer to belt level, an unpleasant thing can happen. Many of the amplifiers used in auditorium PA systems have a sensor that automatically ups the volume of the amplifier if the signal coming in from the mike is too soft—as it would be if you clipped it too low. As a result, not only does your voice get amplified, but so does the sound of your breathing, and in extreme cases, your heartbeat or gut rumble. Every rustle of a tie against shirt, or necklace, gets picked up to be broadcast to the audience. So what is the proper point to clip? If you wear a tie, just below the knot is good, or above the top button on a shirt or blouse.

Some people don't like to use a microphone on general principles. From what I've seen, there may sometimes be a bit of macho in this—"With *my* voice, I don't need a mike." And, to be sure, many such individuals can be heard in the far reaches of the auditorium. The problem is, unless you have had professional voice training, and have the appropriate breath skills, you cannot project a natural-sounding voice to the top of the auditorium. Instead, you shout. Certainly you can be heard, BUT IT IS EXTREMELY TIRING FOR THE AUDIENCE TO HAVE TO LISTEN TO A SHOUTING VOICE FOR 50 MINUTES. This is why I'm a big fan and advocate of good microphones and good mike technique. Your voice actually sounds much more natural when you use a mike, and you can do more things with your voice than if you are in bellow mode.

Once you know you can be heard, even in the farthest reaches of the auditorium, it is time to find out what you sound *like.* For this, you will need a sound recorder. Nothing fancy. Just put it in a convenient place and record an entire lecture.

Next, listen to yourself. Two things you should note: You really do sound like that, and it doesn't sound as bad to others as it does to you (usually). The main value of listening to yourself is to pick up annoying speech mannerisms, not improve the quality of your voice. Without extensive practice or training, you can't do much about the latter, but speech habits are fairly easy to deal with. The most common problem is the use of space-filling words, grunts, or breath sounds. Topping the list is, "unh," which varies in different languages. Other common space fillers are "okay," "like," "well," "y'know," and "now." Add to these throat-clearings and nervous coughing, and you have a possible worst-case nightmare scenario like this: "Well, today, we're unh, going to be, you know, like talking about (ahem) the nervous system, okay?"

When I was an undergraduate at Berkeley, I had a professor who had more annoying public speaking mannerisms in one body than anyone I've ever seen. As I later found out, he was a really nice guy, a tremendous Nobel-quality scientist, and his lectures were very clear and well organized, but experiencing one of his lectures left you glassy-eyed, full of the heebie-jeebies, and not able to remember a single thing he actually said.

He lectured behind a wide chemistry bench. He made sure that the custodian placed a full box of chalk on the stage right of the bench. He would begin by picking up a piece of chalk, breaking it in half, throwing half on the floor, and then making an X on the bench. He would then erase the X with his thumb, and start down the blackboard, writing with his right hand, erasing right behind with his left. I assume he was very shy because he never looked at the class, instead rolling his eyes up so all you could see was the whites of his eyes. Adding to the sensory pleasure was the big wad of spit that gathered in the corner of his mouth. Students in the first 10 rows reflexively wiped their mouths all during the lecture.

When he reached the end of the bench, he would throw the remainder of the chalk on the floor, walk back to the right end of the bench, pick up a new piece of chalk, break it in half, and start all over again. Oddly, one to one, he was nothing like this, and had none of these mannerisms. It shows you what out-of-control stage fright can do.

Students will never tell you that you have habits like that, but an annoying collection of speech mannerisms will definitely distract attention from what you're trying to say. Step one in getting rid of ASMs (annoying speech mannerisms) is to recognize that they exist. That is what the recorder is for. Once you have recognized ASMs, two simple steps will usually dramatically reduce them. First, say to yourself just before you begin talking, "I'm not going to say 'Now!' as a space filler." Say this to yourself a couple of times. Next, slow down just a little bit from your normal speaking pace. This will allow you time to think for just a fraction of a second at the end of each sentence. What you will think is, "Pause, don't say 'Now!'" That slight pause will make you a more dramatic speaker, as well as get rid of the ASM.

Pauses are just as important as words in conveying meaning. Consider Martin Luther King's, "I have a dream" speech:

> I have a dream [one, two, three] . . . that my four little children will one day live in a nation where they will not be judged by the color of their skin but by the content of their character [one, two, three] . . . I have a dream today. [applause]

versus:

> I have a dream that my four little children will one day live in a nation where they will not be judged by the color of their skin but by the content of their character. I have a dream today.

So, when you pause to gather your thoughts so you won't spit out an ASM, your students will believe you are a profound thinker and a dynamic speaker. Moreover, it will be easier for them to keep up with their notes. Not a bad bonus.

Hands

The hands are visual punctuation marks. They are also nervous speakers' worst enemies. Where you put your hands depends on how nervous you are, and how much confidence you have (or can fake).

Putting your hands in your pockets is one way to avoid floppy hands, but if you have something in those pockets, such as keys or change, there is a natural tendency to play with these artifacts if you are a bit nervous. This presents an unseemly visual and auditory stimulus to the audience as you jingle your change.

If you are near a lectern or table, it is a very natural gesture to casually grasp the furniture with one hand, freeing the other for gestures or a handheld microphone. You can also hold notes in one hand, which accomplishes the same purpose.

Another way to totally take your hands out of the picture is to clasp them behind your back, as the British Royals do. Their purpose is to avoid the awkwardness of refusing to shake hands with you, while yours is to conceal shaking hands, but in both cases, a somewhat stuffy appearance is generated.

Sooner or later, as you lose the inevitable jitters that come with lecturing before a large class, you will want to unleash the power of your hands. To do this, you will need to have enough confidence to keep your hands exposed in front of your body. A category of people who are really good with using their hands as punctuation devices are television preachers. Used-car or Vegematic pitchmen are pretty good, too. You'll see that they generally keep both hands in front of them, forearms held horizontally. From this "rest" position, one can easily move to a point where you can say with your hands as you shrug your shoulders, "What can you do?" (hands cocked out, palms up), "Think about this" (tap your head), or pound a palm with a fist for emphasis.

Body

Your students will form their first impression of you even before you open your mouth on the first day of class. Their primary clue will be your stance. Are you confident, arrogant, belligerent, confused, nervous, or comfortable? Right or wrong, they will form these impressions in just a few seconds. Different postures convey different interpretations, and you want to be sure that the impression you actually convey is the one you want to deliver.

Step one is to decide what kind of impression you'd *like* them to receive. Do you want them to know that you're the boss of the course, and what you say goes? Do you want to suggest that you're approachable and friendly? Is it important, as it often is in a pre-professional course, that the students know that you know what you're talking about—that is, you are an authority, but not necessarily an authoritarian?

Once you have made this decision, it is time to choose your stance. Although it is true that interpretations of posture are culturally related, television has acted as a great equalizer. If someone stands before you with his or her hands folded over their chest, depending on whether the shoulders are pulled back or slumped forward, the arms-folded position suggests either a drill instructor chewing out recruits, or a very shy, diffident, defensive person. By contrast, an instructor who strides into the auditorium at the beginning of the hour, having previously set up her notes and visual aids so there is no shuffling at the start of class, will be perceived as an efficient and competent individual.

If you immediately head for the lectern, seeking its security, you will convey a different impression than you would if you took center stage, to the side of or in front of the lectern, and greeted the class as would the master of ceremonies on a TV interview show. In the latter scenario, when you need to refer to notes, you could easily move to the lectern, conveying the impression that the lectern was a place that held notes, rather than a refuge.

Gestures are part of body language and can make an enormous difference in conveying meaning. Gestures are a part of everyday conversation, but onstage in an auditorium, they must be much broader and exaggerated than would be appropriate for face-to-face communication. A good way to see if your gestures are the correct size for the room is to have a friend sit in the back of the room and check you out. Even better is to have the friend bring in a video camera and tape your presentation.

When my department trains new teaching assistants, we always videotape them, and this is the single most powerful teaching aid for showing someone how to make a presentation before a group. It is sometimes brutal to see yourself in this fashion, but it is always instructive. If you allow yourself to be videotaped before a live class, it will be instantly obvious whether your audience will perceive your gestures as tight and constrained (because you were using "normal" gestures) or perhaps over-the-top (because you hadn't quite yet discovered just how broad your gestures should be). Two or three videotaping sessions will make an enormous difference in your stage technique and presence.

Theater

Every auditorium has different characteristics, and when you check yours out before the first day of class, there are two things to watch out for. First, wide and shallow is better than narrow and deep. In the old days, auditoria in classroom buildings were often an architectural afterthought. On my campus, we have two auditoria that could double as bowling alleys. The fewer seat rows there are, the less removed the students feel from the instructor. Newer large classes tend to be built more like a theater in the round, or a surgical amphitheater. This design is great, but you have to be aware that a significant fraction of your class is to your extreme left and right, and you don't want to neglect them as you look around the room. Second, newer is not necessarily better. An older, well-designed room may have better acoustics, sight lines, and "feeling" than a newer one designed by the governor's brother-in-law.

Some large auditoria have stage lights. If yours does, find out how they work, and *use them*. An experience I had with stage lights gave me the first insight that I was an actor and needed to be aware of acting techniques. I was teaching a first-year course in a 1,000-seat auditorium. After class, I would often note a perplexing thing. After I just finished telling students what the important things they had to know were, I would be surrounded by students who repeatedly asked, "What are the important things?" At first, I was annoyed—why don't they just listen? Then I began to think about it a little bit. A teacher is in the communications business. A large fraction of the information that is passed in face-to-face communication is nonverbal. The raise of an eyebrow. A subtle shrug. We form many of our conclusions about the truthfulness of a person by his or her facial expressions. Could it be that perhaps my students couldn't see my face, and thus couldn't pick up the nonverbal reinforcers of my words about importance?

I asked one of my students to stand on the podium in the empty auditorium, and I sat about halfway back. I asked the student to smile. Then to frown. I couldn't tell the difference. In the typical auditorium lighting, her face was a tiny, pink, featureless disc. So I went to the theater department to see what I could do.

The drama teacher I talked to asked me if I had ever seen a theatrical performance where strong stage lights were not used. I couldn't think of a single one. Then she asked me if I'd ever seen a play where the actors didn't use makeup. I truthfully replied that I didn't know. So she told me that I hadn't. In a play, strong light is used on the actors' faces, because at a distance normal room lighting has the effect of making the face look featureless. Makeup is used with the strong lighting to emphasize facial features such as eyebrows. "So, unh," I asked, "could you maybe show me how to use this stage makeup?" She did, and with some trepidation, I made arrangements to have the stage spotlights turned on next lecture, bought some stage makeup, and decided to give it a go.

What a difference. The incidence of students asking "what's important" dropped dramatically. The reason was that I confirmed with my face what my voice was saying. So, as long as I worked that auditorium, I used stage makeup and the lights. As I gained a certain degree of proficiency with the makeup, I discovered you can use makeup to make yourself look better than you really are. I had always admired Robert Redford's (or today, Brad Pitt's) chin line, and with a bit of creme shadow—instant ruggedness! Because I took the makeup off immediately after lecture (and because it was what was known in the trade as "corrective makeup" to compensate for the effects of the stage lights, and was so mild, as makeup goes), students coming up with questions after lecture didn't know I was facially fraudulent. After this brief flirtation with cosmetic self-improvement, I abandoned trying to be more than I was, because I realized that students would start to wonder why Brad Pitt was giving the lecture, but Jack Black was talking to them in my office.

The final thing you will want to check out in the auditorium is where everything is. Where are the light switches, the projector bulbs, the extra chalk, the closest phone for emergencies? It is also a good idea, even if people from audiovisual (or as they like to call themselves these days, "instructional technology") are supposed to set up your projectors and computer, to find out how the instructional technology in your auditorium actually works. Especially during the first weeks of the semester, the student that AV sends to help you out probably knows less about the system than you do, so out of pure self-defense, it will pay to learn about it as soon as you can.

Audience

Freshmen entering a large classroom on the first day of classes come into the room with certain expectations based on their experiences in an auditorium in high school. What happens in a high school auditorium? Regular classes? No. Special events. Rallies. Celebrity visits. Behavior lessons disguised as entertainment (anti-drinking-and-drug campaigns).

So when those students come into *your* class on the first day, look around and see that they are in an auditorium, what are they going to *expect* will happen? Something fun, interesting, stimulating, unusual, and above all, something that doesn't involve work. Now you walk in and tell them that they're going to have to come to lecture every single day, study three hours a night, and if they don't read until their eyeballs bleed, they're going to end up in the fast food industry. Big conflict.

This is one of the reasons why instructors may unknowingly start off on the wrong foot with a big, first-year class. By recognizing that their expectations are different than yours, and taking the time to explain to students that this particular large room is a place of business, rather than a pep rally, you will help them adapt to the new reality.

An audience watching a play has an entirely different experience than a viewer watching the same production on television by himself or with one or two other people. There is an indefinable electricity that makes being part of a crowd a value-added experience. Watching a concert on TV is not the same as being there.

Because most of your students will have had this exciting crowd experience, you can capitalize on that background to turn the class into a dynamic learning environment. Should you choose to be, you can be more dramatic, flamboyant, and yes, even eccentric than you might in a small-class situation, and have this behavior be perceived as "normal"— because the students are in a theater.

However, one of the most woeful sights in the human entertainment experience is a comedian trying to work an audience in a comedy club that is three-quarters empty. In a room designed for a crowd, if the crowd isn't there that space is the loneliest place in the world for a performer. This is why maitre d's place new diners as close as possible when a restaurant opens for the evening. If you have a class of 150, and you are assigned to a 400-seat auditorium, the students will initially tend to maximize the distance between themselves. This is contrary to your purposes. Tell the students in the back to come forward because the acoustics are bad and they won't be able to hear you. Tell the ones on the side to move to the center because the image from the overhead projector is bad on the sides. A few rebels will always want to stay where they are, and if they do, that's fine. However, with the right amount of gentle exhortation, and a few reasonable, if exaggerated pretexts, you should be able to pack them in so that there is only one or two seats between each of them in the front of the room. *Now* you have a crowd, and they will be able to share the magic of being part of an exciting communal venture.

Now you are an actor. You are conscious of the fact that you will require technical skills to reach your class. You know that your class is a crowd and will display crowd behavior. You have learned your lines, practiced them, planned your moves, and checked your costume and props. The audience is in their seats, and they are eagerly looking forward to your appearance. You have a momentary thought that wouldn't it be nice if big-class teachers had sidekicks who would introduce them with, "Heeeeeeeeere's David!" before they came on. No such luck; you're just going to have to do it by yourself. You take in a big breath, and walk confidently out to center stage.

As we superstitious show folk say, "Break a leg!"

4

MANAGING ASSISTANTS AND GRADERS

O Captain! my Captain! our fearful trip is done . . .
—Walt Whitman

One thing graduate school doesn't prepare you to do in academia is to be a boss. And you don't want to share the fate of Whitman's beloved Captain by ending up bleeding on the deck. Large classes frequently involve a staff: readers, lab assistants, lab coordinators, section leaders, and so on. And in the managerial scheme of things, you are their direct supervisor, so when all hell breaks loose, if they have screwed up, you have screwed up, and you will be invited to taste the dishes at the accountability banquet.

We will discuss two main areas: 1) covering your you-know-what (CYA, as the military affectionately refers to it), and 2) getting the most out of your people. They don't necessarily involve the same skills. Doing CYA well usually means that you are managing well too, so there is not necessarily a conflict. Dogbert in the *Dilbert* cartoon is a master at both covering himself *and* managing poorly, but I like to think that he is a bad exception.

Covering Yourself

There are four main areas where mistakes made by your staff can come back to haunt you: 1) Safety: One of your chemistry labs blows up, or a psych experiment goes horribly wrong. 2) Harassment: One of your teaching assistants proposes a grades-for-sex deal to a student. 3) Unfair grading procedures: You receive a complaint from one of your students that your teaching assistant didn't grade her paper according to the course guidelines. 4) General faulty communications: One of your students complains that she asked a question about a question on an examination, and the proctor gave her incorrect information.

In all of these situations a couple of general guidelines apply. First, it is much worse to be negligent than to make a bad judgment call. The same principle that applies to medical malpractice applies to professional malfeasance in academia: If a professionally trained and certified person could reasonably anticipate some adverse action might take place under a common circumstance and failed to plan for such contingency, or failed to recognize a situation that most similarly trained professionals would, and hence dealt with it in an ineffective way—that constitutes negligence. On the other hand, if the situation presented the professional with a difficult choice of actions where the circumstances were ambiguous and the outcome unclear, if later analysis showed that the professional's decision was an incorrect one—that is an error, but not negligence. Negligence is to be avoided at all costs if you are to CYA well.

Obviously, things are a bit more complex and stressful in an operating theater than an amphitheater, but the same ideas prevail. You are not expected to provide direct supervision of your staff at all times—that defeats the purpose of having a staff. What you *are* expected to do is provide training and procedures such that if they are followed correctly there will be assurance that nothing untoward will happen. Then you are expected to provide routine checks to be sure that those procedures are, in fact, being followed. If you can provide documentation that you have provided this training and have established these procedures, with reasonable follow-up, you have pretty much covered yourself.

The best way to protect yourself *and* make sure that there is a better-than-even chance that things will happen the way you want them to is to put everything in writing, even if it is a bit of an extra pain to do so. Your assistants should, at a minimum, have written safety procedures (which are generally specific to a course or a department) and grading principles (specific to a course). They should also be informed in writing about where they can see the college's harassment policies, or be provided with a copy of the booklet, if there is one.

Safety

This is usually only an issue in laboratory or field courses. At the beginning of the semester, assistants should get a general safety briefing and then be briefed on specific hazards before lab sessions that have particular dangers.

Most institutions, at a minimum, will want you to tell your assistants where the location of the closest phone is and the emergency number; the location of safety appliances such as fire blankets, eye wash fountains, and the like; and the location of the first-aid kit. If a staff person in the department is not responsible for regularly checking during the semester to be sure the kit is full, the fountain works, and so forth, then that responsibility normally falls on the course instructor.

For CYA purposes, there is no such thing as a trivial accident. Any incident involving cuts, burns, animal bites, unconsciousness, or unanticipated chemical exposure warrants a call to the rescue wagon. Better to deal with the minor paperwork involved than to deal with a student who suffers a serious infection later from an untreated lab cut. If a student is diffident about receiving such services, the assistant should simply explain that it is standard procedure for all accidents, no matter how minor, and will neither cost the student anything nor require much time. I have found my campus emergency people to be more than cooperative. Because it is a volunteer group, they *like* making calls.

For really minor things (e.g., a superficial cut that immediately stops bleeding) an accident report may not be necessary, but it pays to make sure. Most campuses today have a safety and risk management office, and they can tell you what is or is not reportable. Lest all this sound like unnecessary busy- or paperwork, it cannot compare with the paperwork involved if something goes seriously awry and you *haven't* done the annoying routine stuff.

The U.S. Environmental Protection Agency is taking an increasingly close look at campus policies and procedures on handling hazardous materials and wastes. My campus had to pay a painfully large fine, primarily because there were lapses in paperwork in hazardous materials procedures. If you handle such materials in your courses, it is wise to personally check the work of any assistants assigned to take care of forms.

Harassment

Although interpretations of what sexual harassment is or is not are still somewhat in a state of flux, and the courts now and then provide novel interpretations, the dust has sufficiently settled such that most campuses have some sort of booklet or statement of regulations available concerning the issue. Sexual harassment is considered discrimination and a civil rights violation. In preparing your briefing for your assistants, this is the place to start.

Unfortunately, not all the language in these documents is unambiguous to all people. For example, "offensive" behavior is prohibited, but people's definition of "offensive" varies widely. If a person is offended by food jokes (to take an absurd example) because she is overweight, that might well be grounds for a harassment complaint against an assistant who told an overeating joke. Such a complaint would likely be dismissed, but in the meantime, there would be endless difficulties for the perpetrator. To be absolutely safe, neither you nor your assistants would ever tell any kind of joke, lest it offend; make any kind of compliment, lest it be interpreted in a sexual way; or have any kind of association with a student outside the classroom. You'd be safe but lousy teachers.

Although the wording of these policies may appear to be draconian, local custom and practice can tell you how strictly the regulations are interpreted on your campus and how much latitude an instructor has in his or her dealings with assistants and students.

When I brief my assistants, who are often the same age or even younger than their students, and for whom it might reasonably be expected that Cupid might wish to practice a little archery in their laboratories, I recognize that some significant fraction of my colleagues married their graduate students, and that love eventually laughs at locksmiths. Therefore I tell them that whatever might happen after the end of the term, course policy is that there be no dating during the semester, nor anything that resembles dating—that is, no going to, or leaving with students one on one, even to a professional event, such as a seminar. I encourage them to go down to the union for coffee with their students after lab, but when the crowd thins to themselves and one student, then it's time to go home. I used to be concerned only with male assistant/female student arrangements, but now that the concept of same-sex harassment has been established by law, the course rule applies to any combination.

This is a fairly common practice on many campuses. Some campuses go further and prohibit sexual (or potentially sexual) contact between instructors (as well as teaching assistants) and students evermore. Our campus looks the other way, so I tell the assistants that if they find themselves really attracted to one of their students, fine, but they're just going to have to be a secret admirer until the semester is over; then they're on their own. I don't have any qualms about this because my assistants don't write letters of recommendation for students at any time. If assistants do have this ability, then the issue becomes more problematic because it is conceivable that a student asking an assistant for a letter several semesters after a course was over might receive improper pressure to offer something for the letter. This is, however, much more an issue for faculty than assistants.

In recent years, I have noticed a still rare but very awkward new kind of reverse harassment: older male students coming on in an unwanted way to younger female assistants. I brief the assistants that much of this can be prevented by an appropriate professional manner, but because some of my assistants look like they're about 16 years old, this is a little tough. If the situation *should* come up, the teaching assistants have to deal with it in an immediate, crystal-clear, and forceful way. I tell them to inform the student, in as cold a manner as possible, that they have notified me of the unacceptable behavior, that a continuance of the behavior might be grounds for instant dismissal from the university (not true—the appeals procedure is endless), and the likelihood of their becoming a pharmacist or whatever, rather than a day laborer, is strongly dependent on their immediate cessation of whatever it is that they were doing.

Of course, the harassment regulations all apply to *unwelcome* sexually oriented behaviors. *Welcome* solicitations can be expected when you mix a bunch of young, healthy, randy undergraduates and grad students together. This may not be against either the law or campus regulations, but it most definitely can adversely affect morale among students in the course because there will be inevitable feelings about favoritism, even if there is none. So my policies about nonfraternization apply to both welcome and unwelcome contacts. Something tells me, however, from the number of teaching assistants I see "hooked up" with former students after a semester or so, that this rule is honored more in the breach than the observance.

Grading Procedures

Your name goes on the students' final grade report at the end of the semester, not your assistants'. You, therefore, are the sole determiner of how a student's grade should be decided. However, it may be necessary to farm out part of the grading process to staff, especially in laboratory or recitation sections. Your assistants may not see eye to eye with you on some of your grading practices, and you should certainly listen to what they have to say, but ultimately, the call is yours and has to be something you are comfortable with.

Using assistants for basically mechanical grading procedures, such as multiple-choice or fill-in-the-blank exams that the whole class takes, usually presents few problems. It is where the assistants have some discretion that difficulties arise. The overall guideline, where assistants have discretionary powers, is to assure as much as possible that a student's final letter grade would not be different if he or she were in one assistant's section rather than another, or one assistant read his or her essay exam or term paper rather than another.

Where assistants independently grade essays or term papers, training and standardization can greatly reduce problems. Large-class instructors who give essay or short-answer questions that are corrected by assistants often make up a keyword guide for correcting. If there are five keywords (and/or their synonyms) that the instructor is looking for in an essay, the assistants are informed that five words gets five points, four gets four, and so on. This assures absolute standardization, but unfortunately, you're not really correcting an *essay* question any more—it really is a recall-knowledge short-answer question. If you want your assistants to look for things such as organization, structure, clarity, and completeness—things you would look for in a true essay examination and its questions—then you will have to train your assistants in the techniques I'll show you in Chapter 7 for correcting essays and term papers. These techniques will provide a great deal of consistency in grading from student to student, but your assistants may not be terribly happy with you because they're a lot more time consuming than just looking for keywords or phrases.

If you teach a laboratory course where you have multiple laboratory sections taught by several teaching assistants, you can give your assistants a bit of freedom (and practice) in making up their own questions by simply saying to them something like, "There are 100 total points in lab. I want 50 of those points to be from quizzes, 30 from lab reports, and 20 from a practical exam." You then let them make up their own quizzes. To provide a degree of standardization, have them all compare their quizzes with one another's well before they give them. An assistant who is way out of line, either too easy or too tough, will tend to be brought around to the consensus by peer pressure.

Despite these efforts to standardize, some of your assistants will have more experience than others, and some will simply be more demanding than others. To prevent these differences from having a drastic effect on students' total scores, you can normalize scores between assistants. This is how it works: Let's say we are talking about laboratory sections, and there are 100 points available to students in the labs. Tell each assistant before the semester that they should adjust the difficulty of their assignments such that the *average* score in their sections is as close to, say, 75 points (or in this case, 75%) as possible, but not more than 75. This should be an average across all the assistants' sections. Tell them to keep a running total of their averages so they can adjust the difficulty of their remaining assignments so that by the end of the semester they are as close to (but below) the magic 75 as possible.

Let's say you have three assistants, each of whom has three sections. When the end of the semester is over, one of them has a cumulative average of 74, one 73, and one 72. You give one point to each of the students in the sections of the assistant who has a 74 average. His or her average is now 75. You give two points to each of the students in the sections of the assistant who has a 73 average. His or her average is now 75. You give three points to each of the students in the sections of the assistant who has a 72 average. His or her average is now 75. You have normalized all the assistants' scores, and that should cancel out any differences in grades between sections caused by differences in assistants' grading practices.

There are, however, several difficulties with this scheme that might rule it out for you. First, it assumes that any differences in scores between sections, where the assistants make up and grade their own quizzes, are due to assistants' grading practices. This might not be true. Some sections might have a higher proportion of majors that attract high-caliber students, and thus the sections will have better scores because the students are better. Second, you might have assistants who have trouble easing the difficulty of their assignments and end up with something like a 63 average. When you normalize, the better students will then end up with more than 100%. Conversely, you might have an assistant who has trouble raising difficulty and ends up with an 83 average. Statistically, you could just take eight points away from every student in that assistant's sections, but you could hear the student howls on the moon once the students were told that points were taken away because their assistant was too easy. There are ways that you could perform additional normalizations to compensate for these factors, but the resultant grading scheme would be so complex it wouldn't make any sense to the students. I do a simple normalization and keep regular track of the assistants' running averages so that neither I nor the students have any unpleasant surprises by the end of the semester.

General Communications

A typical problem is a student coming to you at the end of the semester complaining about a final grade and saying that his section leader told him that if he got a certain score in the section, then he would end up with a certain final letter grade for the course. What the assistant undoubtedly failed to mention is that the student would also have to receive a corresponding score in the lecture assignments. Ultimately, this miscommunication is your fault because you didn't adequately communicate what the grading procedures were to your assistant, and you didn't adequately communicate the course requirements to the student. However, if it was stated clearly in your handout material what the policy was, the discussion can end right there.

The best way to deal with this and other problems involving miscommunication is by putting everything in writing *and* having regular (and repetitive, if necessary) briefings with your assistants. In the case just described, a general instruction that students should not be promised definite grades based on their lab scores alone should have been made at the beginning of the semester.

A similar situation arises when assistants are proctoring an examination. If a student asks a question about a question, the assistants will naturally try to be helpful, but they might not have been at the lecture where you covered the material in the question and so might not realize your spin on the subject—and thus fail to give the student your interpretation of the question. These situations can be reduced by going over the examination with the assistants in advance and telling them that if they have *any* doubt about what answer to give to the student, they should contact you during the exam and have you talk to the student.

What happens if you have done all of the above and the assistant either didn't read the written material or was in a fog when you talked about it? Well, this is why the captain is paid extra to make judgment calls. If the student makes a reasonable case *and* when you talk to the assistant it seems plausible that the student was, in fact, misinformed, you might have to make an adjustment. Do you automatically raise the student's grade? No. How do you know that even if the student was informed correctly about the question or the situation, he or she would have done better? What you might do is give the student a second chance to demonstrate that he or she indeed does know the material in question. Give the student a reasonable time, and say that you'll give him or her an oral quiz on the disputed area.

Delegating Authority

If you have 500 students and 10 assistants, you will have to assign responsibility for some decisions to your staff. However, it is very important that they know *exactly* what their discretionary powers are, what your reaction will be if a student challenges their authority, and what they should do if a situation falls outside the guidelines.

A typical situation often arises in grading term papers. The assistants actually read and assign scores to the papers. Invariably, students will compare notes and come to you complaining that they were graded unfairly because a classmate in another section wrote a similar quality paper and got a different grade.

The impact of most such situations can be minimized with forethought. I tell my assistants that if students have complaints about grades they received in a section, they should feel free to come to me, but my role is like that of an appellate judge in the legal system. An appellate judge will never overrule determinations of fact made by a judge or a jury, but will overrule if there have been procedural errors. I tell both assistants and students that because I don't actually read each and every one of their papers, and comparison judging is almost unavoidable in subjective judgments, I am not in as good a position as the assistant to judge relative quality. Therefore, I won't do it. If the student alleges that there has been some irregularity in the procedure of assigning a topic, or some bias in the judgment process, I might overrule, but that's it.

This policy has a number of advantages. First, it gives the assistants a lot more confidence in their decisions, knowing that I trust them enough not to second-guess them. Second, it eliminates a lot of whining complaints. Finally, it is the truth—I really can't judge relative quality without having seen a large sample of other papers, and of course, the problem doesn't come up until after papers have been returned to students.

Does this policy mean that assistants will never make bad calls? No. Sometimes a student will come to me with a complaint, and for the life of me I can't understand why the assistant graded the way he or she did, even with all the standardization training the assistant received. This situation usually arises on an assignment like a term paper, where subjective qualities like "style" are involved. So, do I override the assistant? No, because if I did, I'd violate every principle of delegation of authority. Once word got around, I'd have to look at every student's paper that didn't receive an A. I stick to my policy guns. Needless to say, the student is not terribly happy with me. Then I go to the student's assistant and have an intensive retraining session. When the time comes for the assignment of final letter grades, if I see that the disputed assignment is the only thing keeping the affected student from the next higher grade, I'll use executive prerogative to kick the student up over the line. The result is that it won't happen again with the same assistant, I don't have to deal with a flood of other fishing-expedition complainants, and justice is ultimately done. The student is still unhappy with me because he doesn't know about the last-minute save, but what the heck, you can't always please everybody.

Assistants are informed at the beginning of the semester that there are potentially touchy situations that they should inform me about *immediately* if they come up because it is neither their obligation nor responsibility to handle them. Suspected cheating is one such situation. Others might include a student acting in an erratic manner or having difficult personal problems. Repeated absences. Questionable excuses for absences. Harassment issues. I usually review this list at the first briefing of the semester.

Motivating the Staff

If you have a well-motivated, well-trained staff, you can enjoy many benefits. Your work is easier because your people will do what they're supposed to do, and do it well. Students will think more highly of the course (and you, at student evaluation time). The number of brush fires you will have to put out during the semester will be smaller.

There are no secrets to having assistants get with the program. Common sense and common consideration will take care of almost everything. I usually start the semester off with an icebreaker party at my house within the first week or two of class. Nothing elaborate—just an informal setting for the assistants to get to know me, and one another. When we have an exam grading session, I provide the doughnuts and coffee. I make sure that they are trained in their jobs well enough so that they can approach their classes with confidence.

If you are teaching a first-year course, many of your assistants are likely to be first-year graduate students and may need a bit of hand-holding. Facing a class for the first time is often a terrifying experience, and the more information you can give them in your first meeting, the more confident they will be when that awesome moment comes. If they have all the course procedures and guidelines in writing, their anxiety will be notably reduced.

It is important for them to know early in the game that you are there for support should they need it. Let them know that if there is a difficult or confusing situation with a student, that you will be more than receptive if they bring it to your attention. It's also not a bad idea if you are generally familiar with the bureaucracies they will have to deal with to get their personal life squared away at the beginning of the semester—housing, payroll, registrar, and the like.

You will also need to be aware of the fact that almost all of them will face a conflict between your desires as their teaching supervisor, and their major professors' demands for their time spent on research. At most institutions, it has never really been resolved whether a teaching assistantship is a scholarship or a job (or some kind of monstrous hybrid). The poor assistant is caught in the middle.

It sometimes works out that not all the collective responsibilities, such as grading papers, can be equally parceled out. If that should happen, let the affected assistant know that you are aware of the situation and try to arrange that the next time such an activity comes about, you will assign that assistant proportionately less work.

When all is said and done, your assistants are your *assistants*, not your colleagues. Because you are the accountable person, you are granted reasonable powers to supervise. You don't want your assistants to think that Soc 100 is a landlocked version of the hell ship *HMS Bounty*, but neither do you want them to be able to feel that they are doing you a personal favor by proctoring your examinations. Clear, complete instructions, thorough briefings, explicit expectations, and comprehensive guidelines will go a long way toward making Soc 100, if not the *Love Boat*, at least a happy ship.

5

USING MEDIA EFFECTIVELY

The thing with high tech is that you always end up using scissors.
—David Hockney

Today most people think audiovisual is the place where you check out the projector or find a student to set up your microphones, but 50 years ago it was an educational theory. It said that students can sometimes learn better by seeing pictures and listening to sounds than by reading. Sound familiar? Exactly the same pitch is used today by the multimedia snake-oil salesmen to convince your college administration that they will turn out functional illiterates unless they buy the latest servers and DSL network systems (and the maintenance contracts to go along with them). Like all great sales pitches, this one contains at least a grain of truth. A picture sometimes *is* worth a thousand words. A lousy picture, however, might require a thousand words to explain.

No matter what your subject, you will have some kind of visual communication with your students, whether it be writing on a blackboard or using a computer presentation program. Other than the blackboard, most of your visual communication in a big class will be via a projected image. Much of this chapter will be devoted to getting the most out of that, but first, for the technophobes . . .

The Blackboard

Some of my large-class colleagues still use a blackboard, God bless 'em. And, truth to tell, a blackboard artist can do every bit as good a job with the written word as somebody with PowerPoint and a computer. However, the operational word here is *artist*. It takes a lot more skill to use a blackboard well than to use any kind of projection technique.

In a big auditorium, the major problem is making sure that students in the back of the room can read what you write. Both the width of the lines and the height of the type are important here. For a 100-seat auditorium, your letters and numbers should be no less than two inches high. For a 200- to 300-seat auditorium, double that. For larger than that, don't use a blackboard. The natural tendency when writing on a board is to write in letters about two inches high. That height "looks right" to the writer. That's too small for an auditorium with 200 or more students in it. If you don't believe me, go to an empty auditorium with a ruler, a piece of chalk, and a companion, and check it out.

You will also want to remember that although your students may be young and strong, there is no guarantee that they all have 20/20 vision. As a matter of fact, students at 8:00A.M. classes tend to have lousy vision because, as they've told me, they don't bother to put their contact lenses in before class.

Line width can be increased by breaking the chalk into half-inch lengths and writing with the side of the chalk. A much brighter line can be produced by using what's called "sidewalk chalk," obtainable at toy stores. Custodians hate it because it is hard to wipe clean, and they have to wash the board more frequently. You don't want to have the custodians dislike you or you'll never get your office cleaned, so in the days when I used a blackboard, I'd always wash the board down myself.

Besides visibility of the lines, the other major issue with blackboards is where the teacher should stand in front of the board. The most natural way for a right-handed person to write on a board is to face the board, so he or she can see what is being written. Then, writing at eye level and facing the board, the scribe writes from his or her left to right across the board. This is comfortable for the writer, but does present some problems for the class. First, eye contact with the students is lost. Second, you will be talking to the blackboard, not the class, as you explain what you are writing. This is almost guaranteed to cause their attention to drift. Finally, as a line is being written, the body of the writer passes directly over what has just been written, making it impossible to see from the class, thus defeating the purpose of writing on the board in the first place.

There are a couple of ways around this. Method one is to stand at the board with your right shoulder (if you are right-handed) to the board, as you look over your left shoulder at the class. By twisting your writing wrist a bit to the right, you can then write in more or less normal fashion, but you easily and comfortably look at the class as you write. Your body leads your hand, so you don't cover what you just wrote.

Method two requires more manual dexterity than I have, but I've seen people use it, and it works great. You stand with your back to the board, facing the class. You then grasp a full piece of chalk as you would grab a hammer. Bend your wrist backward, and *voila*, you are writing on the board while facing the class head on. However, when all is said and done, for today's lecture materials, a blackboard is really unsuitable, but some senior lecturers new to an auditorium may feel more comfortable starting with a blackboard then changing to a newer medium later.

The Whiteboard

Blackboards will be historical curiosities in a few years. Almost all new-construction classrooms use whiteboards: off-white, semi-gloss flat surfaces designed to be used with special dry-erase markers. They really do provide a higher contrast image than a blackboard, and once my nostalgia for chalk dust passed, I became a convert.

There aren't any special tricks to using a whiteboard with dry-erase pens, but there is a definite *verboten*. You *must* use the special pens designed for whiteboards. Unfortunately, permanent ink broad-tip marker pens have the same shape and heft, and can be easily confused with a whiteboard pen. Once you use one of these permanent markers on a white board, it is *sayonara* for the board because it is almost impossible to completely erase it. When I use a whiteboard for a class, I keep my board pens as distant from my regular markers as I can, and have made it a habit to check the pens before going to class, just in case one of my students borrowed a marker and put it back in the wrong place.

Optical Overhead Projector

The standard overhead projector for transparencies is as close to a universal projection device for college classes as exists. It has the huge advantage over a board in that you can easily prepare materials in your office in advance—drawings, charts, photographs, and the like. Overhead transparencies are very simple to use, but there are some points to observe.

For one thing, "overheads" almost never receive maintenance from the instructional technology people, so you can take it for granted that the platen—the flat glass part that you put your transparency on—is covered with lines and marks left by idiot colleagues who wrote directly on it rather than using an acetate transparency sheet. Because I am a bit of an obsessive-compulsive about images, teaching a scientific photography course as I do, I periodically clean the platen off with a cotton ball and some alcohol—almost any kind will do. Water (or spit) will take off water-based inks, but not the permanent stuff.

If the overhead is in a room with a chalkboard, the projection lens and mirror are likely to be covered with a fine chalk dust. This gives an ethereal, misty quality to your projected materials, but if you prefer a sharper image, blow off the offending surfaces with some sharp breath puffs, then *gently* use a clean handkerchief as a duster. Don't use paper towels or facial tissues for this purpose because both can scratch the lens. Don't use alcohol as a cleaning agent because it can seep through to the cement that holds the lens elements together, dissolving it and giving you really cool 1960s light-show images.

Unlike computers, which can offer a thousand opportunities to improvise during a critical performance because they lock up, freeze, and so on, an overhead projector can only play one dirty trick on you—it can burn out its bulb. Naturally, this only happens when you have a sheaf of drawings on acetate sheets that absolutely cannot be transcribed to a blackboard.

The prudent instructor thus needs one simple skill, and one simple artifact—a spare bulb. Some projectors have a backup bulb and socket built in, but because no one ever informs instructional technology that a bulb has popped, and they have switched to the secondary, you may safely assume that when you lose a bulb on a two-bulb machine, it will be the second one that has given its life in service.

Life is short, and a relatively small expense can save a world of aggravation. I eliminated all worries about whether the person in the class before me walked off with the community microphone by buying my own. Following the same logic, I bring my own overhead bulb to class. Twenty bucks, and I can sleep like a baby.

Changing bulbs is usually straightforward, but all machines are different, and it is a good idea to practice before need. Some projectors now use halogen bulbs, and you must not get any fingerprints on this kind of bulb. Halogen bulbs are usually quite small and are wrapped with foam rubber in their package. Handle the bulb by the foam while you plug it in, then gently pull the foam off.

Legibility

The real issue with overhead projection, or any other kind of projection media, is whether students can see, read, and understand what you are putting on the screen, even if they are in the back of the class. If the projection facilities in auditoria were properly designed, this would not be as much of a problem as it often is. The screen would be so large that the magnification of the projected image would take care of an original whose text was too small. However, projection is often the last item to be considered in auditorium design, and we have to work with projection screens that are too small. For example, in my auditorium, which holds 450 students, according to generally accepted projection standards the main projection screen should be at least 13 feet wide. It is, in fact, 10 feet wide, and the size of projected letters is thus almost one-third smaller than it should be.

What this means is that when preparing materials for overhead projection, either by copying printed material or handwriting, the error should generally be on the conservative side, and the letters should be a bit larger than you think they need to be. The following guidelines will get you started.

The "8x" rule applies to almost all media that will be projected. It says that if you hold your original (acetate sheet, color slide, laptop screen) about eight times its height away from your eyes, and you can read it from that distance, it will be okay if it is projected following the *other* set of rules for projection that auditorium designers should follow governing how far a projector should be from a screen. For example, an acetate transparency sheet is about a foot high. If you take your finished overhead transparency, prop it up against a wall, and look at it from a distance of eight feet, that will give you a pretty good idea of what your students will see from the back of the auditorium after it is projected. You will immediately see that if you copy a chart, spreadsheet, or text from an article or book directly to a transparency using a copy machine, the students won't be able to read it.

Similarly, if you hold a 35mm color slide, which is about an inch high, about eight inches from your eye, that will tell you what it will look like when projected. Look at your laptop screen, which is about a foot high, from a distance of eight feet, and that will be about what the image will look like from the back of the auditorium after it is projected.

As a demonstration, prop this book up, stand eight times the height of the book away, and look at the following type:

This is 11 point.

This is 13 point.

This is 17 point.

This is 22 point.

What is the minimum size you can read?

In practice, this means that lettering on the original that will be copied as a transparency needs to be at least a quarter-inch high. Typical 12-point type, which is the default size for most word processing programs, is about half the size needed for legibility when the paper original is copied to a transparency in a copy machine.

If you will be preparing originals using a computer, then printing to transparency film in your printer, bypassing the copy machine, the problem can be solved by simply changing your font height to, say, 24 points.

You won't be able to get as much information on the page, but your students will be able to read what you present.

If you want to use a copy machine to make your transparencies from a printed sheet or book page, most machines will allow you to make enlargements of about 150%. Naturally, you will not be able to get an entire 8.5 x 11 original on an 8.5 x 11 transparency with that degree of enlargement, but you can in effect zoom in on the important chart or table on the page. An enlargement by 150% is not really enough for legibility—200%–250% would be better—but it represents a decent compromise.

Now, all this assumes that the joker who designed your auditorium knew what he or she was doing when the projector lens was picked and the projector set in place. This often doesn't happen, so in terms of lettering, bigger is almost always better.

You can make a crude but effective kind of animation with an overhead projector by making a "sandwich," using four or five (but no more) sheets of transparency material. Let's say you wanted to demonstrate an organizational chart. On the first transparency you would have:

The big boss

On the second sheet, you would have:

Tape the two transparency sheets together on the left edge. Project the bottom one and talk about bosses, then flip the second one over, and you will have:

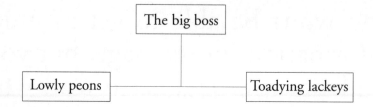

These overlays are a nice way to demonstrate a complicated process that proceeds in steps. Another way to accomplish more or less the same thing is to prepare a single transparency that has the whole process, then cover over each of the steps with pieces of taped-down paper or masking tape. Pull them off as you reveal each step. I prefer the overlays because once they're made they're pretty bulletproof, but the little pieces of paper are always falling off between lectures. The technical term for this method of presentation in graphic arts circles is *progressive disclosure.*

35mm Slides

With the advent of computer-based presentation programs such as PowerPoint, the trusty old 35mm slide has just about disappeared. However, slides still have a number of significant advantages. First, the projection facilities required for them are simple and reliable, something that can't be said about computer projection systems. I don't know how many seminars I've attended where Windows has gleefully decided to lock up just as the speaker begins the presentation. Second, where the texture and detail of the projected image is important, as in art history or anatomy, 35mm slides are still far superior to computer-generated methods, although that advantage is disappearing. Third, slides are relatively permanent—I have Kodachrome slides that were perfectly good for classes 30 years ago, and they look the same today as they did then. It is extremely unlikely that an electronic presentation made today will still be usable 10 years from now, due to both deterioration of the medium ("disc rot") and obsolescence of the computer platform. Finally, 35mm slides are universal and portable. There is scarcely an academic location in the world that doesn't have a

35mm projector. A box of slides is a lot easier to carry around than a laptop and less likely to be damaged or stolen.

Kodak has stopped making 35mm projectors, but the old ones are pretty sturdy and still easily repaired. There are only two skills needed to deal with almost any kind of perversity the machine might throw at you. First, you need to know how to change the bulb. The exact technique depends on the model but usually involves nothing more than undoing a thumbscrew on the bottom of the projector, opening a little hatch, lifting a wire lever, and pulling out the old bulb. At the beginning of the semester, I buy myself a bulb (about $20) and if a bulb burns out, one minute and I'm on my way again (unfortunately, slide projectors and overhead projectors generally use different bulbs, so if you use both kinds of projectors, you need two bulbs).

If a slide is bent, or an old cardboard mount slide has frayed edges, it is possible for a slide to jam in the projector. You thus need to know how to unjam a Kodak projector. It is a lot easier to do than to describe, so I'm going to refer you to whoever is the oldest member of your school's information technology group to give you a briefing. This information can make you into a hero at meetings and seminars. Very few people today know the secret of unjamming a slide projector, even the students at AV, so just when panic is about to break out, I yell, "*I* can take care of that!" You can pick up significant gratitude points this way.

Preparation of Materials for 35mm or PowerPoint Slides

In the old days, "artwork" (charts, tables, graphs, outlines, etc.) destined for reproduction as auditorium projection slides was prepared by a graphic artist. In most cases, faculty had neither the training, time, nor talent for such work. You just told Ken, or Robin, what you wanted, in maybe 20 seconds of conversation, and a week later there was your artwork. Today, however, graphic artists for such academic purposes are an endangered, if not extinct species, and faculty, who still have neither the training, time, nor talent, are expected to do their own artwork, thereby saving your college a salary and only lengthening your workday by an hour or so a day. Such is progress.

If you will be projecting 35mm slides of things that one would usually use a camera to produce—landscapes, photographs of paintings, people—then you just pop your processed slide into a slide projector and away you go. However, if you want to have a text or composite slide that combines text with images, you will have to become a graphic artist of sorts, and the usual way to prepare such artwork today is not by using illustration board, rulers, and pens, but a computer and "presentation software."

Graphic Considerations for Projection

Although PowerPoint is the most widely used presentation software, it is neither the easiest to use nor the best in terms of the attractiveness of the product. I find Corel Presentations to be easier, and it has more variety of templates or basic slide layouts. The only catch with using something other than PowerPoint is that you pretty much have to use your own laptop because most computers won't have anything except PowerPoint loaded up.

I will be referring to two kinds of "slides." The first is a real, physical object: a 35mm slide. The second is a virtual object: one frame in a computer presentation, also sometimes called a "slide show." There are devices available that you can hook up to a computer that let you compose a frame in PowerPoint, then use the device to make a 35mm slide. These are rarely used today, and most people compose a frame in PowerPoint, then project it in PowerPoint. In either case, your very first step in setting up your frame (either for conversion to a 35mm slide, or direct to PowerPoint [or similar]) is to tell the program you are using what *aspect ratio* you want. The program may use a different term, like *format* for this value, but aspect ratio is what it is—the relationship between width and height. A computer monitor is about 4 units wide and 3 units high (in the case of the monitor I'm using right now, that's about 11 inches high, and 14 inches wide). This would be expressed as a 4:3 aspect ratio. A 35mm slide has an aspect ratio of 3:2. "Widescreen," now becoming commonplace for video, is 16:9. What this means in practice is that a 35mm slide or widescreen is quite a bit wider compared to height than a normal computer monitor. The practical effect is something like what happens when a widescreen movie gets "formatted" for television—they have to chop the sides off. In our case, unless you tell the program to use the format you will eventually use for the final product—3:2 to eventually make a 35mm slide, or 4:3 for

PowerPoint—the program would have to chop off some of the top and bottom, or both sides. However, if you *tell* the program that your final product will be 35mm slide or widescreen, it will give you a working area just right for whatever aspect ratio you will be using for projection. The program should ask you about this at the very beginning of the preparation of your slide show.

There is a kind of cheating that we sometimes see now on widescreen computer monitors or TV screens, including the new high-definition models. If they are confronted with material originally prepared for a 4:3 screen, instead of chopping off the top and bottom (sometimes called "letterboxing") to produce a 16:9 projected image, the device will electronically "stretch" the image. The most noticeable result is that people's faces and figures are fatter. Not grotesquely so, but definitely different.

Once you have established your aspect ratio, how much "stuff" can you pack into one slide? In the words of the architect Mies van der Rohe, "Less is more." Here's a handy guideline to get you started. Take a 35mm slide with text on it and hold it at arm's length up to a light. If you can read it with the naked eye at arm's length, your audience will be able to read it when projected. Shocked at how big the type has to be to be legible? If you go to professional meetings where slides are used, either 35mm or presentation software, you will see that the vast majority of slides are *not* legible to people sitting in the back, or even in the middle. Remember, however, that the purpose of slides at a meeting is to impress your colleagues with how much data you have (and if your data is a little shaky, to prevent an unpleasantly close examination of same). In a class, by contrast, students actually have to be able to read what is on the screen with some degree of accuracy.

The original legibility guide for text 35mm slides that are oriented in "landscape" mode (wider than tall) was no more than nine lines of type. That is not much information per slide. Most of the pre-made templates for slides in the presentation programs adhere to this guide. When amateurs like ourselves (as opposed to professional graphic artists) prepare text slides from scratch, we tend to cram in as much information as possible, going to smaller type sizes to get every last bit of data in. If it is not important that viewers actually *read* the slide—if the purpose is more to give some sort of visual or emotional effect, or a general impression—

then type size doesn't matter. However, these graphic arts standards have been developed over generations of use by professionals in the field and have pretty much stood the test of time.

Typefaces

There are two major styles of type: serif type, such as this one (Times New Roman), that has little pedestals at the top and bottom of the letters, and **sans-serif type, such as Arial, which is simpler and without pedestals**. In general, serif types are easier to read as part of text, and sans serif are more eye-catching, especially in larger sizes. Because there should not be much text on a slide, sans-serif type is usually preferred for text slides. It is tempting to mix type styles on a slide for "interest," but the result is usually choppy looking.

Computer Presentation and Projection

Most auditoriums these days have some sort of computer projection facility. Electronic projectors have improved dramatically and have come way down in cost over the last couple of years. They still have an approximate lifespan of 4–5 years (compared to 10–15 years for a slide projector) and must be electronically aligned every six months or so, lest strange and marvelous colors appear where none were intended. You, however, will need a few vocabulary terms to earn the respect of the techies that you will inevitably have to talk to when you project electronically.

A general purpose electronic projector is called a "multi-scan." The electronic signal from a videocassette recorder is not the same as the one from a computer, and the first electronic projectors could handle a TV signal or a computer signal, but not both. The first multi-scans would let you change between one or the other by throwing a switch, but the current generation of projectors does the switching automatically. If your auditorium has only an older video projector and you want to project from a computer, you are not dead, but you will need a black box called a "scan converter." A scan converter will let you feed the output from a computer into a TV set or older video projector, but there's a big loss in quality of the image—even nine lines of type might be too many. Fortunately, scan converters have almost joined the brontosaurus.

Computer presentation programs started to come into fairly wide use in the early 1990s. Laptop computers were not nearly as common as they are now, so if an auditorium was set up for computer projection, there was a permanently hooked-up Mac or PC or both. You prepared your frames in your office, slapped them on a floppy (or later a Zip disc or CD), slipped it into the computer in the auditorium, and . . . prayed.

People rapidly discovered that using a computer that other people had used had about the same appeal as using somebody else's tooth-brush—you didn't know where it had been or what was on it. The last person to use it might have changed all the preferences for the desktop, buried the shortcut to your presentation program, and if you were naive enough not to write-protect your disc, left you with a little souvenir to bring back to your desktop computer. It also turned out that the presen-tation programs were surprisingly machine—and program-version—dependent. What might look fine on your machine would be hash on the auditorium's machine.

Thus, many early adopters, like yours truly, got burned and pulled away from computer-direct-to-projection classroom media. Now, howev-er, the laptop has come to the rescue. Our auditorium-specific comput-ers are candidates for the computer museum now. Today, you just bring your laptop to class, hook it up to the auditorium's projector through your serial port (which is already being replaced with something faster, such as a USB or FireWire connector), and away you go.

What about graphics standards for computer-direct projection? It is pretty much the same situation as mentioned earlier for 35mm. When you start preparing your slides in your presentation software, the default aspect ratio will be for computer projection, typically about 4:3 so you don't have to worry about it. To see if what you have prepared will be leg-ible in class, just stand eight times your monitor's height away from the screen and check it out. If you can't read it at that distance, your class can't read it when it is projected.

Scanning, Resolution, and Format

One way or another, if you are going to have computer-based projection of images of book pages, printed photographs, or three-dimensional objects, you will have to somehow get the image into the computer. It is getting easier to do this with each generation of image-processing software, but you will have to resign yourself to learn a little bit about how images are handled by computers. The exact how-to details are specific to programs, but the following general observations will help you make some sense of the program's instructions.

There are three basic sources of images that you can feed into your computer:

1. *An already-digitized file.* This might be something you pulled off the web, or an image from a digital camera.

2. *Flat work.* A photograph, a magazine article.

3. *Film.* A negative or a slide. Each requires a different kind of handling.

A digitized file contains an image that has already been digitized by somebody. These files contain varying amounts of information that will influence the final appearance of the picture as it is projected. Generally, picture files that are uploaded to the web are intended to be viewed as a relatively small image on a computer screen. If you pull such a file off the web, then greatly enlarge it for projection, you may be disappointed with its quality. If the person who originally digitized the image had in mind that it would be significantly enlarged, he or she would have stored it at a higher *resolution*. A given picture size can be stored at different resolutions. Why not store everything at the highest possible resolution? The higher the resolution, the more space it takes on a disc, and the longer it takes to upload or download.

Image files are stored in a variety of formats, and the lack of standardization will bedevil you as you learn to handle digitized images. Images that are captured and stored in one format may not be easily read, or read at all, by the program you are using to assemble images for presentation. The different formats are identified by initials, and you may see things like GIF, JPEG, PDF, or TIF after the name of a picture file. Fortunately, one format, JPEG, is emerging as a standard format for pictures intended for the web, and most presentation programs can incorporate JPEG images without difficulty.

"Flat work" describes source material that you might have that is . . . flat. A photograph, a drawing, a page from a book are all flat work. The device one uses to digitize flat work is a flatbed scanner. Flatbeds have come down remarkably in price, and they're now so cheap that if you have the desk space, they're a realistic adjunct to your personal computer. The image capture software that you will need to operate the scanner comes bundled with the device. Higher price will bring you greater scanning speed, ability to store files at higher resolution, better color accuracy, and ability to handle larger flat work. If all you will be doing with your images is using presentation software and a computer projector, you don't need the capacity of an expensive machine. When you scan an image, the machine will ask you in what format you want to store it. The best, all-purpose compromise (IMHO—in my humble opinion, as the computer folks say) is probably JPEG, until you gain some comfort with the system.

If your source material is 35mm slides or negatives, there are two possibilities. Some midprice flatbed scanners have film adapters that let you use the flatbed for slides or strips of negatives. This is only a so-so solution because flatbeds do not inherently have the high resolving power necessary to do a good job with a film original. If you want a good-looking digital image from a film source, you will need a film scanner. These devices have four to five times the resolving capacity of a flatbed. Unfortunately, they are much more expensive than a flatbed, and thus are usually found only in a department or instructional technology center. If, however, you are in a field such as art history or appreciation, where the quality of the projected image is important, and you want to go digital, it will pay to hunt up a film scanner. If you have a lot of slides to digitize, you need to know that film scanners tend to be much slower than flatbeds, so be prepared for a substantial time investment.

Electronic Overhead Projector

We now come to a truly marvelous gadget, the only one of the new instructional technologies that actually *saves* instructors time. It is called variously a "visual presenter," "electronic overhead," or often, and to the distress of the trademark holder, an "Elmo" after the brand of one of the more common ones. All it is is a little television camera with a zoom lens that points straight down at a translucent piece of plastic that can be illuminated from beneath. There are a couple of small fluorescent lights that can also illuminate the plastic plate from above. The output from the camera gets fed into the auditorium's TV projector or multi-scan projector.

You can use your collection of overhead transparencies that you have been using for years. No problem—just use the set of lights under the plastic plate. Do you have a transparency of a giant table with 400 cells that created a great general impression but was impossible to read? Fabulous! Show them the whole thing with the lens set on wide-angle, then zoom in on the critical bits and they will be crystal clear with the push of a single button.

An interesting article in the newspaper today? Cut it out, bring it in, slap it on the plate, use the above-the-plate lights, and there it is. No scanning, no using the copy machine to copy it onto transparency material. Real time. Zoom in on the important parts.

Want to talk about frogs today? Why be content with a picture of a frog? Bring in a frog! Slap him down on the plate and tickle his toes. The presenter can handle three-dimensional objects easily. Blinded by the light on a conventional overhead projector? No bright lights here.

Such an amazing machine must have some drawbacks. Absolutely. The image is neither as bright nor as sharp as the one produced by a conventional overhead projector. However, the latest generation presenters, coupled with a similar projector, come very close. The zoom feature largely neutralizes this disadvantage. Also, although the zoom lens can blow up a 35mm slide, the magnification is at the limit of the machine's capacity, so the image quality is not nearly as good as that of the same 35mm slide projected in a slide projector.

Of all the new educational technologies, this is the only one that I can't imagine getting along without. It even has a bonus—my handwriting was terrible when I wrote on transparencies on a conventional overhead, and I had to write unnaturally large to compensate. With the presenter, I write on paper, with my favorite pen, crank the zoom up a little, and the students can read my writing for the first time in my 38 years of teaching big classes.

If your auditorium has a video or multi-scan projector and you don't have one of these things, call in all the favors you can from your administration and get one. It can give you back some of the hours a week that computers take away from you.

Live Television

This falls into the category of "not for everybody," but it has worked very well for me, and my students almost universally like it. Medical schools have been pioneers in developing and using this technology. About nine years ago, when we remodeled our auditorium, putting in a multi-scan projector and all kinds of electronic switches so we could move back and forth between a computer output, videotapes, DVDs, presenters, and the like, we decided to also include the capacity to use studio TV cameras. The idea here was not just to have a "talking head" that could be piped to another room to take care of overflow from the auditorium. Rather, it was to make the auditorium class experience more like what a TV studio audience experiences, or what rock concertgoers experience, where the performer is live, and in the flesh, but you can actually see his or her face from the back of the auditorium, on the big studio or arena screen.

It required a fair investment in cameras and associated equipment, and it has the continuing expense of a camera operator from AV, but after all who were concerned more or less mastered how to use the equipment, and how to *teach* using the equipment, I'd have to say it was quite successful, due to a unique property of the TV medium.

When somebody, a reporter for example, looks into the lens of a TV camera, the viewer has a pronounced feeling that the reporter is talking to *them* and them alone. When I look into the lens, every student in the class, including the ones in the back and to the side of the room, thinks I am addressing them personally. From the back row, when viewed with the naked eye, my face is just a disc, with no discernable facial expressions. With the TV, they can see the slight raise of an eyebrow, the tiny shrug that conveys nuance to what is being said.

When combined with the presenter, the result is dynamite. I can use split screen, where what I write scrolls under the picture of the speaker, so the students don't have to look at the live speaker, then up to the screen, as they have to with a conventional overhead. I can use "blue screen"—the "weatherman" effect—where it looks like I'm standing in front of whatever I'm talking about (a cell, a liver) pointing out its features.

The method required a difference in stagecraft. Whereas a stage actor's gestures have to be larger than life, the TV actor's gestures and expressions have to be smaller than life, lest they look hammy or exaggerated.

I won't claim it was easy to learn how to do this. We couldn't afford a "director" who would tell the camera operator what to do and switch back and forth between the various cameras, so I'm the director. Not only do I have to try to remember what my lines are supposed to be, I also have to be thinking about what's on the screen now and what's going to be on next. For the first year or so, it was worse than the fictional amateur cable TV show *Wayne's World*. Now, it's not the Discovery Channel, to be sure, but a lot better than local access cable.

A bonus and incentive for faculty to learn how to use this technology, and administrators to financially support it, is that it is a natural lead-in for distance education. Distance ed means working in front of a camera, which takes a fair amount of practice to learn, and such a class whose home site was a real, live classroom, instead of a cramped, primitive TV studio would be very attractive to potential distance ed students.

I've persuaded a couple of my colleagues to try it, with mixed success. One extremely outspoken colleague looked like a deer in the headlights for a whole hour, and said "never again." Another, who is normally quiet and retiring, *loved* the camera, much to my amazement, and is now a worse ham than I am. So you can't really tell in advance.

The Internet and Web

There are a variety of ways you can incorporate the Internet into large-class teaching. The simplest is email. For small classes, email can be a godsend, but the larger the class, the sooner your mailbox will fill overnight. Most of this traffic will be queries about the time for the exam, what was the reading assignment for the week, and so on. Occasionally, you will get a perceptive question or two. For shy students, email can be very beneficial because they might be too intimidated to make direct personal contact with you. I provide my email address in the course handbook but don't verbally encourage students to contact me (nor do I discourage them), and find that I have a manageable volume of mail. I have found that students expect a reply to their communiques almost instantly, and if you are slow to answer your email, you might find yourself drawing some heat from students who are looking for instant service.

Many auditoriums now have a network outlet on stage, and you can hook up to the Internet directly and interact with web sites right in the class (assuming you can hook your computer to an appropriate projector). Some of my colleagues swear by this technique, but unless the site you are connecting with has a very fast response (and your campus network is also fast), you can spend an inordinate amount of time waiting for a download while the class twiddles its thumbs. Whenever possible, I try to download anything of interest from the site in advance to my hard disk; then I can have almost instant response.

For more ambitious Internet use with a class, there are a variety of packages available, the most widespread of which is WebCT, that allow you to store course-specific files or programs on the web and have your students access the information 24/7.

A perusal of courses using WebCT on my campus suggests that the primary use for the system at the moment is to provide electronic handouts—things we used to distribute on paper but are now downloadable. Undoubtedly these uses provide a convenience for students—they don't have to come to class or see you if they lose their syllabus, for example—but I haven't really seen a "killer application" that is qualitatively better than what can be done in class, or what used to be done with paper. In fields that make use of practice problems, such as chemistry, the problem sets can be done online. It is also possible to have the students do graded homework assignments with the system, but there is no guarantee that a student completing a graded assignment from his or her dorm room doesn't have a little assistance from friends. Students make heavy use of the "chat" feature, when it is enabled by the instructor, and although much of the chat has little to do with the course, some students use it to quiz and/or help one another. It is illuminating to eavesdrop in the chat room after you have given an examination. You might never have heard yourself described in quite that fashion before. A few brave souls have made custom presentations or animations, but these take an inordinate amount of time to produce.

If your campus is not set up with a system like WebCT, several of the large commercial text publishers have proprietary course programs that will let you do the same things. If you adopt their book, they will give you a password that will access the system. If you do use such a system, I suggest you check its functioning very carefully before making your course dependent on it. Computerized test banks supplied by publishers were very useful when they first came out but are now often riddled with errors, and the publisher-supplied online resources seem to be following suit.

Clickers

The newest development in large class technology is "clickers"—small handheld radio transmitters the students can use to answer questions posed by the instructor with his or her laptop, somewhat like the audience response devices on *Who Wants to be a Millionaire?* A number of the major publishers now bundle these systems if you adopt their text for your class. The system consists of a program disc that you upload to your computer, a tiny radio receiver that you plug into a USB port, and the transmitters, one of which is shrink wrapped with each new textbook. Bookstores will typically buy back the clickers, along with the books, at the end of the semester, so there then is a secondary market for clickers in subsequent semesters for students who buy used textbooks from alternate sources. Unfortunately, there is not yet standardization among publishers and clicker systems, and the clickers are sometimes not inter-changeable. It *is* possible that if you adopt a new textbook, you might also have to revise your clicker presentations.

The program is essentially PowerPoint with an extra toolbar. You make a slide show in which each frame is a multiple-choice question with up to 10 potential answers. You put the question up on the screen, and the students have a few seconds to push an appropriate answer button on their clicker. The program shows you a running total of number of responses, then after the answer period is over it shows you the fraction of students answering each alternative, and it shows the student the correct answer.

Along with transmitting answers, the clickers also transmit an individual identifier code, so you could actually take roll with the things. You can also split the students into teams and invent game shows. I use them to get demographic information about students—how many had high school honors biology and so forth.

There was a fairly steep learning curve because, like PowerPoint itself, it has the capacity to do far more things than any sane person would want to do, and you have to wade through all that stuff to find, for example, the "change slide" button.

I can see myself using the system more, rather than less, especially as a lecture break technique.

Images, Time, and Some Philosophizing About Media

Multimedia today means that you combine still photographs, video clips, sound bites, and text together to assail the student with information from a variety of sources, all cobbled together in a presentation program that students can either operate themselves in the comfort and squalor of a dorm room, or which you can narrate and provide color commentary for in a class situation.

I have yet to see any good studies that show that an average multimedia program is better than a terrific conventional lecturer, but I would be the last to argue that a class about the civil rights movement wouldn't be improved by having the students listen to Martin Luther King's "I Have a

Dream" speech against a background of pictures of Selma and Birmingham. What rarely is mentioned however, is how much *time* it takes to prepare a multimedia or straight video presentation. A general rule is 1:1: an hour or more of your time for a minute on the screen. Even the simplest production can take a prodigious amount of time.

This was rubbed into my nose when I first started to think of my class as a lively yet educational television show—I realized that every episode of a show on TV has opening credits. So I would need title slides, with pictures appropriate to the lecture. I wanted them to be professional looking, to go with the impression I was trying to convey with the class.

To go beyond the standard templates for such things that come with PowerPoint, I had to learn some very user-unfriendly professional image programs, such as Photoshop. Unfortunately, these programs are so complex that if you don't use them every day, you forget all the commands, so if you haven't used the program for a month, it is *not* like riding a bicycle—a lot of things have to be relearned over and over.

Then comes the dirty little secret. Once you learn how to use these things, they are *fun*. I still recall making a title slide for "Non-Linear Biology." It had to have exactly the right image, the right layout, be eye-catching, and say "Wow!" So I started looking on the Internet for a good central image. "No, this one's not right. Close. This one's good, but I have to take out the background, and then maybe splice it onto . . ." I was totally engrossed in the project and finally finished with a sigh of satisfaction. I glanced at my watch. Four hours. I had just spent four hours making one lousy title slide, and the fact that I enjoyed every minute of it raised some questions for which I still don't have answers.

Were my students going to get four hours of *educational value* out of my time investment? How much more would they get out of watching this fantastic title than if I had just written "Non-Linear Biology" on a blackboard and spent that time updating my lectures, designing new laboratories, or even talking to a few of them one on one in my office?

I wrestled with this question for a long time. However, I have noticed that with each passing year, my students have come to *expect* more and more flashy graphics because that is what they have been surrounded with since birth, and I realized that perhaps my question was based on a false premise. It is not so much that the multimedia stuff is *better* than a textbook-and-spoken lecture model, to someone who grew up with reading as his major medium of information transmission. It is rather that many of these students can't handle a conventional approach, and we have to deal with them in ways that are comfortable for them, not us.

I realize that it sounds like a capitulation—the students can't read, so we won't ask them to read. Their attention span is short, so we won't ask them to do anything that requires sustained, focused attention. That is not what I'm saying, however. We simply have to recognize that the educational experience our current students bring into our classes is very, very different than our experience at their age.

Even in my small honors first-year classes, I find that many students' knowledge of formal English is rudimentary. When I correct their papers, I have to explain things to them that I learned in 10th-grade composition class about which they have no clue. In four and a half months, three hours a week, I can't bring them up to speed on *everything* they should have learned over the previous 12 years. But I can, and should, try to catch them up as best I can on the basic tools of learning and communication that they have missed, while at the same time presenting new information to them in a form that they can not only handle, but handle expertly. I guess what it all means is that "spare time" for teaching academics in the future will be something that will be remembered fondly, like IBM Selectrics (typewriters—some of you are probably too young to remember them) and secretaries.

Murphy's Law and Using Media

A piece of chalk is not a terribly effective teaching tool, but on the other hand, not much can go wrong with it. A PowerPoint presentation can take your breath away, but it would take half a dozen paragraphs to list all the things that could go awry with it, from a program crash to a hard disc failure, to a burned-out $900 bulb in the projector. Computer systems are not yet refrigerators, so the prudent large-class instructor realistically *always* has to have some kind of low-tech backup for the inevitable. At a minimum, this probably ought to be a lecture outline with a tickler list of terms and concepts you want to cover. After spending 10 or more hours making a 50-minute PowerPoint presentation, such an outline would only take you an extra 5 or 10 minutes. Also, if there are critical drawings or drawings in the presentation, print them out as transparencies, or if your printer won't handle transparency material, print out a hard copy and make a transparency copy on a office printer so you will have something for the overhead projector. It's a small price to pay for big insurance.

6

AUDITORIUM CLASSROOM ACTIVITIES

For Satan finds some mischief still
For idle hands to do.

—Isaac Watts

In 1965, I took Don Abbott's summer invertebrate zoology class at Stanford's Hopkins Marine Station in Pacific Grove, California. The class started at first light, about 5:30A.M., at the Great Tidepool. We would be blindsided by giant waves and pinched by grapsoid crabs until 7:30, then retire to a diner for "Adam and Eve on a raft" (poached eggs on toast) and a cuppa joe. Don would start lecturing at 8:00. The first five-minute pit stop came at 10:00, followed by another at 11:00, and we would break for lunch at noon. At 1:00, he'd pick up the chalk again and go until 3:00, then we would have lab until 6:00. Those were the days, my friends, and you may have had similar experiences.

Those days seem to be gone forever. I am sure that somewhere there are undergraduate students today who could maintain that kind of focus, but I tend not to see many of them in my classes. Over the last 10 years or so, I have found that the traditional 50-minute lecture on a topic that is not "fun" for students has become increasingly difficult for them, and my colleagues who teach the hour-and-twenty-minute lectures used for three-credit courses that meet twice a week report that it is nearly impossible. Their attention wanders, they chitchat, their eyes glaze over, they fidget, and sometimes they just get up and leave.

There are a variety of reasons why our students seem to have a much shorter attention span than in days of yore, but for our purposes they are almost irrelevant—we have our students for 50 minutes, and we have to make sure that the maximum amount of learning takes place in that time.

Straight Lecture Equals Death

What it comes down to is that 50 minutes of straight narrative talking to them doesn't seem to work anymore. By the end of the period, they're absorbing very little that you're saying and are squirming in their seats. So, is the traditional lecture dead?

Not exactly, but it needs to be thought of more as a television show than a one-act play. In a half-hour TV show, there are 22 minutes of content and 8 minutes of stuff that pays the bills. Whatever the format—comedy, drama, action—it is all written so that there is a natural "break" in the narrative every 7 minutes. The narrative is written such that if you come in in the second or third segment (because you were channel surfing) it is easy to pick up the flow of the story. This makes for terrible drama but an interesting challenge for the writer. It is also a format that our students have been exposed to for tens of thousands of hours since they were infants. In their email, IMing, and texting, they are also used to very short forms of discourse.

Breaks

In my experience, a class can follow an instructor for 20–25 minutes without too much loss of attention. More than that, and large numbers start to drift. What this means is that if you then put in a short "commercial" break or two where they're doing something, anything, other than listening to you and taking notes, you can pick up their attention again. The trick is to make this one- to two-minute break something that is educationally useful and complements the traditional narrative part of the hour.

When I first started putting in these breaks, I wasn't terribly happy about it. One or two minutes per lecture means that you've lost a whole lecture's worth of content over the semester. However, once I fine-tuned the activities and saw how beneficial they were for the students, even beyond their function as a lecture break, I wondered why we hadn't done these things in the old days.

One of the simplest of these break activities can also be highly illuminating for you. When you come to a natural stopping point in your presentation, tell the students to pull out a fresh sheet of paper. Then tell them, "Write down the three most important things I said in the last 25 minutes. Be prepared to read them aloud." Give them 45 seconds or so, then start calling on them. You will discover that the phrase "most important" may mean something very different to you and your students, as I discussed in Chapter 2.

After the first time we do the exercise, I have an excuse to talk about "important things" and what they are. I emphasize that they have to *listen* to the lecture, not just transcribe it. It takes some practice for them to get the hang of this. After 8–10 of these exercises I can see a marked increase in their ability to generalize and synthesize.

The next step after this simple activity is to ask them to sit next to a partner, write down the three most important things individually, then negotiate with the partner until they can agree on at least two important things. Then I call on individual groups to name off one of their important things. A remarkable amount of learning takes place in these little negotiating sessions. There is also a bonus because they know that if I call out this activity, and they've been sleeping or off on Mars someplace, there is a certain embarrassment potential when they have to compare lists with a partner.

As an alternative to this activity, I sometimes ask them to write down a question for me, or to tell me about something they think is confusing, then pass a note forward. A disadvantage of this activity is that the "passing forward" creates a bit of a distraction as you're trying to get rolling into the second half of the presentation. Also, a smaller fraction of the class seems to want to participate than is the case with the "most important" list.

When I get the stack of papers up front, I quickly scan through them as I talk, and if I see there are several similar questions, or one that strikes my fancy, I'll wait until the next natural break in the lecture and see what I can do. I tried having students leave the questions at the end of the lecture for me to review and prepare for at leisure, but I found that by the time a couple of days went by, they were ready to move on to the next topic, and unless the question was really compelling, or I had large numbers of the same question, indicating that I had screwed up an explanation, the moment had passed and I would have to spend too much time reviewing the background for the question.

Quite a few of the questions you get essentially ask you to repeat what you just said. This is more a function of inattention than confusion, and I have usually refused, in a polite way, suggesting that they check a friend's notes.

Nowadays, I also use the clickers mentioned in Chapter 5 for a class breakup. Before class, I make up a simple clicker-style PowerPoint presentation that includes a half-dozen questions. Students seem to enjoy it, and it takes about a minute to deliver.

The Mock Jury

Once you have established the rhythm of a break somewhere in the middle of your lecture, the sky's the limit on the kinds of different activities you can have. I've found that several activities that one thinks of in the context of a discussion in a small class can also work in an auditorium, with a bit of adjustment.

One of my class's (and my) favorites is the mock jury. There are many areas where biology intersects the law: DNA fingerprinting, carcinogens, reproductive issues, to name a few. To get ready for such an activity, I'll try to find a court case that has something to do with the topic I'm currently teaching. On the day of the activity, I'll tell the class to form themselves into six-person juries. This is easiest done with three students in one row, and three in front of them. They'll have to bunch up to do this, so unless the class is packed, there will be a little space between the juries. I then give them the "scientific" part of the presentation, a summary of the facts of the case, the prosecution and defense arguments, then turn it over to the "juries." This activity usually requires more than a minute; depending on the case, they can come to some kind of closure in three to five minutes. I explain to them that juries must come to a unanimous conclusion, or else be hung. I also tell them that they have to keep their voices down, or there'll be chaos.

Once the case goes to the "juries," I'll walk the aisles, eavesdropping and asking the occasional question. They get a couple of time alerts, then

I tell them they have one minute to come to a conclusion. I'll then ask the "foreperson" of the jury to stand, and I'll go around the room asking for verdicts. If I've done a good job, the guilty verdicts will just about match the not-guilties, or in a civil case, the plaintiffs will win about as often as the defendants. This presents an ideal opportunity to then ask what additional information might have caused the juries to come to verdicts that were more similar.

Games

In recent years, especially in my nonmajors' courses, where I am not under as much pressure to deliver "content"—that is, facts—in class, I've had a lot of fun with game-show activities during lecture time. "Biology Jeopardy" is a perpetual favorite. Students play for grades rather than money. It is structured in the general way the real TV game is played. Four students to a game panel. There are two rounds of play with five categories of 10 questions each. The questions are in increasing order of difficulty and value. I've been too lazy to make up the button and buzzer used on the show, so students just raise their hands.

Students are selected for the panel by preliminary rounds of tryouts. Out of a class of 250, I'll typically get 40–50 students who try out. There are two levels of tryout. The first is essentially a written quiz. This winnows them down to 10 students. There is then a mock game outside of class to select the panel.

The prize? The winner gets a guaranteed A in the course, regardless of his or her exam and lab scores. Number two gets a guaranteed A–, three a B+, and four a B. If, say, number three has an A– by virtue of his or her exam scores at the end of the semester, they get the higher of the two letters. Pretty good deal.

The game takes half a lecture period, and I usually have it about three-quarters of the way into the semester. I first started doing it because *I* was bored with straight lectures and wanted to do something different. I didn't really think there would be much educational value for the class as a whole, although clearly it was beneficial for the participating students.

After trying it, however, I was amazed by how many students tried out for the game, the amount of work the participants did, and the buzz in the class. They were talking about it for weeks in advance. This led me to an observation: Many students today, particularly freshmen, will work extremely hard for a shot at a "bonus," and almost not at all to avoid a potential penalty. The threat of a bad grade has little resonance with students who went to grade-inflating high schools; very few students in college prep tracks ever really receive bad grades.

The enormous popularity of two recent TV shows, *Survivor* and *Who Wants to Be a Millionaire?*, offered other opportunities for game activities. *Millionaire* proved to be easier to adapt for class use. We changed it to "Who Wants to Be an 'A' Student?" Individual students are challenged to answer a graded series of increasingly difficult multiple-choice questions. This is all done in class. The student and I sit on stools facing each other, and one of my teaching assistants puts the questions on the overhead projector. They go through five giveaway questions to warm up. If they get the next one right, they get a guaranteed pass. If they get the next one, they get a guaranteed D+ regardless of their regular exam scores, and so on up the scale. If they answer the next eight questions correctly, they get a guaranteed A in the course. Like the TV show, they have three kinds of "lifelines" if they are stumped by a question. In one, they can ask the audience. We do it the low-tech way with a show of hands, but next time I try it I'll use the clickers mentioned in Chapter 5. The second lifeline is 50–50. I throw out two of the possible answers. The third is ask a friend. They can invite anyone they want to sit in the front row and be an expert. Each kind of lifeline can be used only once.

There is a fair possibility of cheating, with confederates in the audience providing signals, so we dim the houselights and use bright stage lights. The audience is then almost invisible from the stage. We have two "break" points at C– and B. For example, once they have a C–, on subsequent rounds, if they aren't sure of the answer, they can walk away from the question and get their highest award. If they get it wrong, they drop back to a C–.

Unlike the TV show, there are time limits for each answer because I don't want any one contestant to take up more than 10 minutes of lecture time. The nice thing about this kind of game is that you can do one on fairly short notice, for example if you are in a draggy part of the semester and students have other things on their minds, such as vacations.

These kinds of activities can easily be overdone. Many students would be delighted if you dispensed with lecture altogether and had nothing but games. However, the amount of content you could present would drop to zero. I use them sparingly, like just the right amount of seasoning to provide interest to a nutritious but otherwise unstimulating dish.

Whether it is a game, a "what's the most important thing" break, or a jury, these little activities can help you reach students who are not quite ready for a full uninterrupted hour of college lecture and have them do something useful with that break time.

7

ASSESSMENT AND TESTING

Suppose a man is able to recite all three hundred of The Poems, but when he is given a position in the government he is unsuccessful. Suppose he is then sent on missions to the various states, but proves unable to think for himself. Even though he may know many poems, why continue to employ him?

—Confucius

Testing and the assignment of grades will require more thought, can cause you more grief, and will cost you more time, semester after semester, than any other aspect of large-class teaching. It also has the potential of causing a significant amount of stress, as you undoubtedly will have to deal with some disgruntled students at the end of the semester. On the other hand, a good testing and grading system is a powerful teaching tool that can be used to motivate students.

It's unlikely you'll get too much assistance from more experienced faculty on how to set up your testing and grading policies. Academics often have very strong opinions about grading, but discussion of grading in academic circles is very much like discussion of religion in the outside world—if you're going to have to work with other people on a close and regular basis, even if you have definite opinions on the merits of your religion and the deficiencies of others, it is best to avoid the topic altogether.

There are many sources of information available on the theory and practice of testing and grading, most intended for elementary and high school teachers, or education faculty. I will list some of these later, and concentrate here on practical aspects.

Assessment

In recent years, a new buzzword has appeared in the professional education community. *Assessment* activities are those an instructor conducts to get an idea about how the class is doing *before* students are formally evaluated. Assessment is aimed at the needs of the instructor, rather than the student.

An example of an assessment would be a pre-test you would give students at the beginning of the semester to see how much information they remembered from high school (or how badly they distorted it). Students wouldn't put their names on the sheets, and you would primarily be interested in group statistics. Another example of an assessment would be to ask students to submit questions about the lecture to you in writing. This is an activity that can give you an approximation of what fraction of the class is having troubles with a given topic.

The advantage of doing regular and frequent assessment activities is that you can make midcourse corrections using the information you get and fine-tune your presentations. A quiz or exam can give you similar information, but if an explanation was unclear, it's too late for the students.

There are a couple of factors that will influence how often you can perform assessments and what you can interpret from them. The biggest problem with paper-based assessments such as pre-tests in large classes is the hassle of dealing with that volume of paper. If you have a question about something that can be answered yes or no, or can be categorized, a show of hands will do, or you can use clickers for a bit more sophistication, but if you want to know what aspect of your explanation is causing problems, then you must allow the students to write their answers out, and bite the bullet about processing the answers.

How you word your assessments can be important in how you interpret the results. If you simply ask, "Did you understand X?" you will receive many negative answers. This is because students are smart. They know that the more time you spend on X, the less the likelihood that you will have time enough to talk about Y and include it on the next examination. They also have the intuitive and probably correct feeling that the more time you spend on a topic, the greater the likelihood that they will eventually do well on exam questions on the topic. On the other hand, if you ask, "Is there anything about X that is still confusing, and if so, what specifically is confusing?" you will receive fewer answers, but they will be more useful to you.

Assessments can also be used to tell you about attitudes in the class. "What are three things you like about the laboratory?" coupled with "What are three things you dislike about the laboratory?" can give you more information than "On a scale of 1–10, rate the laboratory." The problem with such numerical evaluations, whether they are on an assessment or a faculty evaluation, is that you don't know what to do with the information once you have it. If the laboratory received a rating of 3.7 out of 10, you can be reasonably sure that the students didn't like the lab and something will have to be done, but you don't know *why* they didn't like it, and so where do you go from there?

Testing and Grading

Testing is determining what a student knows and how well he or she can use that knowledge. *Grading* is assigning a student to a category, based on some measurable attribute, and will be covered in the next chapter.

The two main concerns in testing are validity and reliability. A test is *valid* if it actually measures the thing you are trying to measure. It is *reliable* if you give it to several groups or different individuals who have the same relevant characteristics, and it produces reasonably similar scores— that is, it produces consistent results.

It is surprisingly difficult to produce a valid test when different kinds of learning are factored in. Often college teachers believe they are testing a student's understanding of a concept, when in fact the student may simply be demonstrating a virtuoso memory and have little or no understanding.

Reliability is easy to measure in a theoretical sense, but difficult to measure in practice. For example, if one lecturer had several lecture sections, he or she could administer the same examination to both sections, and look at the scores. However, it's guaranteed that the scores in the second section would be higher because questions and their answers are all over the campus within milliseconds after the completion of an examination. Classes that meet at 8:00 are very different than classes that meet at 10:00, and even if they have the same composition of majors, year in class, and so on, they are likely to produce different exam scores, even on the same examination.

To produce a valid examination, you must know before you write the test what kinds of learning you want the students to demonstrate. Any text on educational psychology will have extensive discussions on types or levels of learning, and some of the schemes are quite complex. For many years, I have used a simplified hierarchy of learning that is easy to translate into questions.

Levels of Learning

Memorization

Simple memorization is part of the foundation of many disciplines, and it is both necessary and appropriate to test a student's memorized knowledge of such things as vocabulary and definitions. "Who were the combatants in the Gulf War?" "What is the name of the largest bone in the forearm?" "What body establishes federal interest rates?" Simple memory questions can be expressed in a variety of formats and levels of difficulty.

Short answer:
    State the laws of thermodynamics.

Multiple choice:
    Who wrote The Catcher in the Rye?
    A. Pierre Salinger
    B. J. D. Salinger
    C. Yogi Berra

True or false:
    California is bigger than a cockroach. True_____ False_____

The difficulty arises when an instructor is *trying* to test a student's higher order understanding, but the question permits the student to give a memorized answer. I had a nice demonstration of this when I was making the rounds in one of my laboratory courses. The students were dissecting frogs, so I pointed to one of the frogs' kidneys and asked, "What is the function of the kidney?"

"The-function-of-the-kidney-is-to-remove-impurities-from-the-blood," was the reply.

Well, that happens to be the textbook answer, and if that had been a short-answer examination question, I would have had to give the student full marks. But the way the student said it suggested he understood what he was saying about as much as a parrot would. So I next asked, "So, it removes impurities? Suppose we gave the frog a diet that had no impurities—fresh, organic flies, no pesticides, nothing impure. Would the frog still need a kidney?" No answer. The student had memorized a phrase from the book but had no understanding of it.

Even an extensive answer might be totally memorized. In an economics class, if you asked the student to "Explain Keynes's economic theory," you might get back three pages essentially straight from the text, and you would have to give it high marks. If instead you had asked, "Explain today's downturn in the stock market in light of Keynes's economic theory," and you got a well-reasoned answer, you could have a lot more confidence that the student actually understood the theory.

There is no real trick to writing memory questions in any format. The challenge is making sure that if you want to test understanding, the question doesn't permit a memorized answer.

Translation

A translation question is one where the student is asked to transform information from one form to another. Changing tabular information to graphical, word problems in mathematics to equations, or technical language to layman's language are all examples of translation tasks.

Some specific examples might include:

Prepare a pie chart showing the distribution of sales of the following fruits:

Kind of Fruit	Percentage of All Fruits Sold
Mango	25
Ube	33
Rambutan	42
Total	100

From the following graph, in what quarter was the smallest number of porgy sold?

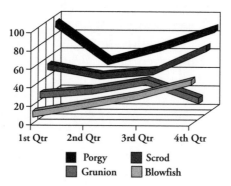

Testing for the ability to transform information is straightforward, with two caveats. First, if a translation task is part of a larger process that is being tested, don't automatically assume that students have that skill. For example, graph reading and graph preparation skills are often deficient in first-year students. If these skills will be important in solving problems in your area, make sure that students come into the course with these skills, and if they don't, resign yourself to teaching them.

Second, if you have taught the transformation skill in your class and you want to test if your students are proficient in it, don't use an example on the examination that you used in class. Students are quick to memorize an example, rather than analyze it, and if you use a class example on an examination, you are likely to be testing memory rather than ability to transform.

Concept Formation

Concept formation is a buzz phrase from the educational literature and essentially means what we usually call "understanding." Does a student understand a principle—how it was derived, how it works, how it relates to other principles, and what its properties are? Thus, an answer to the question "Explain the second law of thermodynamics" will not necessarily tell you whether the student actually understands the law—a perfect answer might simply be memorized from text or notes. In contrast, "Which of the following situations shows the second law of thermodynamics in action?" would reveal if the student understood the mechanism of the law.

It is not quite as easy to write a concept-formation question as it is to write a memory question. If it is your wish to test understanding, questions that start with the words *explain, discuss, state,* or *describe* are likely to produce memorized answers. On the other hand, if you ask the student to recognize an example of the principle from a range of nonexamples, you are more likely to detect whether the student actually understands the concept. For example:

> Which of the following provides an example of a
> negative feedback loop?
> > A. A Colt .357 Python
> > B. A flush toilet
> > C. A bunion and a grunion
> > D. A bottle of Budweiser

The correct answer is B, which leads to some potential hazards in this kind of question. If, while explaining negative feedback loops in class, you had used a flush toilet as an example, showing how the water level returns to the same point after each flushing, the student would be able to answer the question by memorization, rather than concept formation. What you *hope* the student would think is something like this, "A negative feedback loop is a process that can be used to maintain something constant in the face of external fluctuations. Colt Python? There's nothing inherent in a revolver that demonstrates a negative feedback loop. A flush toilet? The water level in the tank comes back to the same point every time you flush the toilet and drain the water out of the tank. That meets the definition of a negative feedback loop exactly. B it is."

A couple of things make writing this kind of question tricky. First, the student has to have a basic understanding of what the alternatives are and how they work. If the student didn't know how a flush toilet worked, he wouldn't be able to recognize it as an example of a negative feedback loop. The second problem is more insidious. One of your really bright students might be able to see a relationship of the kind you're looking for in one of your incorrect answers. This is a little far-fetched, but a student might argue for C: "A guy who has a bunion is walking on the beach and steps on a bunch of grunion [for those of you with no familiarity with the West Coast, grunion are small marine fish that come to the beaches by the millions to breed; "going at it like grunion" is thus an old California expression]. Grunion are very oily fish, and his bunion would have gotten worse because of all the walking he did, but it stayed the same because the grunion oil soothed it. Q.E.D., it's a negative feedback loop." *I* used bunion-grunion as an incorrect alternative because I thought the words were funny and rhymed, and certainly had nothing of a negative feedback loop about them. The student was able to see something I didn't. This is the kind of thing that drives the people who write analogy questions for SAT and ACE nuts. The only real way to guard against this is to use *distractors* (a distractor is educational jargon for the wrong answer in a multiple-choice question) that are so far-fetched that even the most creative student would be hard pressed to find the correct relationship. Unfortunately, that tends to make the question easier, so a balance is needed.

Application

It is one thing to understand a principle, it is quite another to be able to apply it in practice. Application might involve a whole constellation of skills beyond simple understanding. There is a big difference between understanding how a watch works and being able to repair one.

Testing for application is easy. Just give the student a problem to solve using the principle under examination. An example:

> A mother whose blood type is B gives birth to a child whose blood type is A.
>
> The blood type of the father could be:

A. Only B
B. AB or O
C. B or AB
D. A or AB
E. B or AB

If an initial loan amount is $100,000 and the compound interest rate is 6.7% a year, what will be the total amount of interest paid at the end of three years?

A patient was admitted to the hospital suffering from the following symptoms: irregular heartbeat, chronic indigestion, and slurred speech. After a series of tests, a neurologist was called in for a consult. She concluded that the patient had possibly suffered injury to one of the twelve cranial nerves. Which one?

In all of these examples, it is important to note that there is a *possibility* that a student might give a memorized answer to what is intended to be an application question. For instance, in the blood type question, if mother type B/child type A had been used as an example in lecture to explain the principle, the student could simply have memorized the example and give a correct answer to the examination question without understanding the principle at all.

In application problems, there is a fairly straight line between the statement of the question and the production of a single answer. A more challenging type of question, requiring another level of learning, is complex problem solving.

Complex Problem Solving

Outside the world of tests and examinations, problems are rarely simple or straightforward. There may be too much information, or confusing information, or unreliable information. It may not even be clear what the problem is: " My computer is giving me the Blue Screen of Death. What is it *this* time?"

We would like our students to take what we teach them and be able to use that knowledge somewhere in their lives. The ultimate test of both teacher and student is: How well does the student do in a real-life situation, where he or she must decide on an appropriate approach to the problem, select a method of solution, and then successfully apply that technique? The case study approach in business, design problems in architecture and engineering, and literary analysis in literature all represent examples of complex problem solving. By their nature, there is no one correct "answer" to tasks such as these:

> Produce a model economic development plan for Costa Rica.

> Write a short story around the theme of the betrayal of a friend.

> Given a budget of $140,000,000, what is an appropriate bridge design for a channel 2,400m wide, depth of bottom 31m, with hundred-year winds of 240km/h . . . ?

Answers to such questions tend to be lengthy and not amenable to a keyword grading system. They are very difficult to write in a multiple-choice format, although standardized examinations such as the Medical College Admission Test and Graduate Record Examination have multiple-choice questions that come close to testing this level of learning. However, for day-to-day teaching, valuable as they are, these kinds of questions are difficult to incorporate into large courses, especially introductory ones where students might have a lengthy list of basic terms and novel concepts to deal with.

Types of Examination and Quiz Questions

The kinds of questions you write will depend on the level of learning you're trying to measure and the practicality of administration. The size of the class will be a strong determinant of the kinds of questions you can ask. For questions of factual recall, a multiple-choice question is appropriate, easy to administer, and amenable to machine scoring. Even if you are a glutton for punishment, correcting 300 true essay exams by yourself is neither practical nor educationally sound—it would simply take too long to get the results back to the students and the grading would be inconsistent.

For midsize classes, it is often both possible and desirable to have a hybrid examination: one or two essay or short-answer questions, the rest multiple-choice (or similar) format.

Essay

A "true" essay examination would be evaluated on its composition, organization, quality of argument, and presentation. It would also be impossible to give a memorized answer to it, as might be the case were the question "Explain Gresham's Law." Unfortunately, it is rarely feasible to spend the amount of time necessary to fairly evaluate answers to such questions in a large class. It is also very difficult to maintain grading equity in evaluating such questions in a large class—by the time you come to grade an answer from student number 235, which is almost identical to number 98's answer, you will have forgotten how you scored it and end up giving different scores to the same answer. Because students always compare notes, this can lead to awkward and embarrassing situations.

Some instructors nevertheless take pride in asking essay-type questions in large classes. However, to make it possible to grade such a large number of answers, especially if there are readers helping to grade the examination, they prepare a keyword guide—a point apiece for mention of important terms or phrases. The structure, organization, or writing quality are necessarily ignored.

Such a practice essentially converts a "true" essay into a "pseudo" essay question, which is little more than a fill-in-the-blank. These pseudo essays are faster to correct and produce more consistent scores than true essays, but they don't really test the students' writing ability.

I would be the last to argue that a true essay question isn't better than a multiple-choice question at assessing higher order learning, but in large classes, sometimes you just can't ask such questions. I get around the problem a little bit by telling my large-class students that the "default" examination format is multiple-choice questions, but if any individual feels that his or her knowledge would be better demonstrated with essay questions, all he or she has to do is let me know a week before the examination, and they can have either an oral or essay examination. Whereas it might take 5–10 hours to write a really good multiple-choice examination, an essay exam can be churned out in minutes. I find that about 1% of my students ask for an essay examination, and I have had one request for an oral exam since I started giving them the option 20 years ago. As a bonus, giving them the option eliminates a lot of grousing at the end of the semester—"Oh, the reason I did poorly in biology is because I never do well on multiple-choice examinations!"

"Really? Then why didn't you ask for a different kind?"

Matching

Matching questions are good for testing up to and including concept-formation levels of learning. In a matching question there is a column that has a list of words, ideas, definitions, and so forth, and a similar column to its right that contains words that are somehow related to those in the first column. There are two basic subformats: one in which the terms are physically connected by lines (which is cumbersome to correct), and a second in which a letter from the second column is placed in a space next to a number in the first.

A	B
__1. John Steinbeck	A. *The Moon Is Down*
__2. Henry Miller	B. *Justine*
__3. The Marquis de Sade	C. *Nexus*
__4. Sylvia Plath	D. *The Brothers Nostradamus*
	E. *The Bell Jar*

You want to have unequal numbers of alternatives in the two columns because if the numbers are the same, if you get the first ones right, you automatically get the last one right, jacking the scores up. The subformat shown here lends itself to machine grading.

Short Answer

The short answer calls for a single sentence or at most a short paragraph. It is amenable to keyword correcting, hence useful when graders or readers will help you correct. The short answer is useful for demonstrations of memorization, but rarely used for higher order thinking. The exception is numerically oriented fields such as mathematics or engineering, where a succinct answer might require a great deal of thought.

Fill-in-the-Blank

This kind of question presents students with a sentence having a missing word and invites the student to fill in the blank. It is useful for testing *recall* memorization, rather than the *recognition* memorization demonstrated in a multiple-choice question. The only real pitfall is that halfway through correcting the examination, you might find that a very creative student interpreted the question differently than you did and legitimately put in a word that you hadn't imagined. This is not much of a problem if you're doing all the correcting yourself—you simply give the student (and any subsequent students who have the same answer) credit. If you have graders who are less familiar with the field than you are, they might not allow an answer you would, and you might have to deal with a post-examination argument. One way to partially circumvent this is to scan through a selection of completed exams before you turn them over to graders. You then have a chance to spot these renegade answers and modify the answer key you give to readers before grading begins.

True-False

By guesswork alone, a student will get a true-false question right 50% of the time. If passing is 60%, that means that a student doesn't really need to *know* very much to pass a true-false examination. If that is what you *want*, fine, because that is what you will get. It is possible to knock down chance scores by deducting wrong answers from right, rather than just counting right answers, thus discouraging guessing. I am reluctant to do this because half of my research publications started out as lucky guesses and I don't want to discourage "educated" guessing, but many of the standardized testing organizations, such as Educational Testing Service, often will discourage guessing, so it is a legitimate technique.

Another difficulty I find with this type of question, at least in my discipline, is that so few things are *always* true or false that I find it to be very limiting. But such questions can add fill or padding to an examination and are certainly easy to correct.

Multiple Choice

Multiple-choice questions are the de facto standard for large-class examinations. They can test learning at all levels, from simple memory to complex problem solving, and are amenable to machine scoring. They are subject to a number of difficulties in their writing, however, and you need to be aware of them.

Due to the wondrous complexity of the English language, a question that may seem absolutely straightforward to you might draw a legitimate, different interpretation from a student. This is not a problem with simple "Which of the following is the largest bone in the wrist?" questions, but if you are testing higher order learning, such as application or complex problem solving, you might end up with two possible correct answers where you were originally sure there was only one. A way to deal with this is to have several other people read over *and take* the exam before you send it off to be printed. I make my teaching assistants take the exam at our regular assistants' meeting. I cannot say they like to do this. I say, "What's the answer to number one?" then go around the circle. I have a large stock of soothing comments to minimize their embarrassment should they miss something a sixth-grader should know. Every time I do this process I ferret out at least one question that needs to be reworded. The assistants know that a bad question will cost them time in the long run through recorrecting the exam, so although they grumble, there's no serious resistance.

A second problem with multiple-choice questions is that the exact wording of higher order learning questions is critical. You can demonstrate this yourself by asking a question this semester, recording the fraction of the class that gets it right, then asking the same question with a slight rewording the next semester you teach the course. Many times you will find a significant difference between the two. Thus, if you want to "salvage" a good higher order learning question for later use but change it slightly between semesters, you may find a different fraction of the class answering it correctly.

Many textbook publishers today will include a computerized test bank for instructors as an incentive for adoption of a book. The questions are mostly in multiple-choice format. When these were novel and provided a competitive advantage to publishers who used them, a considerable amount of care went into their preparation. Now that they are an *expected* part of the adoption package, I have found a fair amount of sloppiness has slipped into the test banks. Common glitches include mismatches between the answer key and the question, having a question about a topic discussed in one chapter included with a different chapter in the question bank, and errors in grammar and syntax. I initially refused to use questions out of a test bank for reasons of professional pride, then I realized that for routine, boilerplate questions, I actually could save some typing time by using bank questions that were essentially the same as ones I would write myself. Now that I have to scrutinize each question closely and check to see where exactly in the text the source material for the question is located, a lot of the time advantage has evaporated. *Caveat emptor.*

Before one writes multiple-choice questions, there are two decisions to be made. The first is, What are the conventions about questions you want the students to assume? A widely used convention is that a "correct" answer is both true in all its parts and relevant to the question. For example, if the question is "What color is the moon?" an answer of "Cheese is made of milk" would be incorrect, because although true it is irrelevant to the question. Another convention is often that there is only one "correct" answer to each question. Thus, A and B could not both be correct unless there was a D alternative—"A and B are both correct."

The second decision is, How many alternative answers do you want to have? Students can guess answers, and if you don't discourage guessing by some sort of right-minus-wrong scheme, if you only have three possible answers, a student can score at least 33% right off the bat by guessing. So a passing score on a three-alternative exam would not really indicate that a student knew 60% of the material, or whatever you use as a minimum passing score. Four alternatives cuts the correct-guess possibility to 25%, and five chops it to 20%. However, once you go past four alternatives, it becomes increasingly difficult to come up with additional plausible but incorrect answers. Four possible and two wildly improbable answers do not a six-alternative question make. Four to five alternatives represents a reasonable compromise.

Educational theory suggests that a multiple-choice question should only address one specific point—a term, a phrase, a numerical answer, and so on—because if the question calls for the student to get several ideas correct to give a correct answer, how do you know which one the student got correct and which one he or she missed? The point is valid, but if I can only ask multiple-choice (or similar) questions because my class is so huge, I want to be able to identify those students who not only can demonstrate bits of knowledge, but can also put things together.

The only way to do that is to ask questions that have some degree of complexity. True, I may not know why a student who got it wrong, got it wrong, but at least I have found some students who got it all right. Clearly, you would not want all of your questions to be complex, but to be sure that you don't give As to students whose only claim to excellence is an excellent memory, you *need* some complexity in a few of your questions.

It is possible to add complexity to a multiple-choice question by structuring it so multiple answers are possible:

> Which of the following animals have wings?
> A. Bird
> B. Butterfly
> C. Baboon
> D. A and B
> E. B and C

One could criticize this structure by pointing out that if a student gets it wrong, you don't know exactly why he got it wrong. If he answered E, perhaps he knows for sure that a butterfly has wings, but he doesn't know what a baboon is and took a chance. The response to the criticism might be something like, "I want to know if the student knows that both birds and butterflies have wings. I can determine this with one question, rather than asking separate questions about bird wings and butterfly wings, thereby saving a question for another topic."

"All of the above" is sometimes used as a distractor. The only problem with this is that on a five-alternative question, if the student knows at least two of the answers are true, the others must be true, too, because there is only one "correct" answer possible. Where "all of the above" is the correct answer, it is an easier question than it might seem to be.

"None of the above" is also sometimes used to stretch the number of possible distractors. This structure tests students' recall as well as recognition memory, but a clever student may well think of a better answer than any of yours:

> Which is the largest mammal?
> A. Pig
> B. Rat
> C. Elephant
> D. Shrew
> E. None of the above

The instructor might have had in mind "elephant," but a marine-minded student might well think of "whale" and thus check E. If the instructor had said "land mammal," or "on this list" then the difficulty would have been avoided.

Most large-class instructors today use machine-corrected multiple-choice examination forms, but if you will hand-correct, there are a few points to keep in mind. Students should be instructed to use capital letters only (A, B, C, D, E) because a handwritten small *a* looks too much like a *d,* leading to ambiguous answers.

To reduce the possibility of cheating, the answer sheet the students fill out should have small spaces for answers, using a small-type font:

> 1. __   5. __
> 2. __   6. __
> 3. __   7. __
> 4. __   8. __

A student glancing at a neighboring paper would have to strain very hard to see these answers.

When you type up a hand-corrected answer sheet, leave as much space between the answer columns as possible. You can then make a "window" key for correcting. Physically cut out the paper between columns on a blank answer sheet. You will end up with something that looks like a hand, with the "palm" containing the instructions to the exam, and the "fingers" containing the columns of answers. Fill in the correct answers in the appropriate spaces. Now, all you have to do is lay this key over a student's answer sheet, and his columns will be right next to your answer columns. You can mark off incorrect answers accurately and quickly.

Item Analysis

If you have your multiple-choice exams machine-corrected, you can often get a statistical package with your corrected exams showing a histogram, mean, standard deviation, and something called an "item analysis." This lets you look at several things. First, it identifies the number of students who answered each alternative on a question. If a huge number of students all got the same wrong answer, perhaps there was something wrong with the wording of the question, or the students just don't understand the idea and you might have to revisit the topic. Second, it splits the class into two groups: those with high scores and those with low scores. It then looks at the fraction of the high group that got a given question right, versus the fraction in the low group that got it right. Ideally, the good students should have a much higher fraction of correct answers than the low ones. If they don't, and the distribution of correct scores is about the same between the two groups, the wording of the question might have been confusing to the better students, or even the good students didn't understand the principle that was the basis for the question.

In extreme cases, you might decide to throw a question out on the basis of the item analysis. You really don't want to have to do this too often because it means recorrecting everyone's exam. Alternatively, you might decide to re-cover the material in class, or reword the question if you use it again in future semesters.

When I first started using machine-corrected exams, I was a big fan of item analysis and found that it did sharpen my question-asking skills. After a while, my experience and intuition pretty much told me everything I needed to know, but if you are just starting out, I can heartily recommend using item analysis.

Evaluations Other than Tests

If you are teaching a large class without assistance, it is difficult to evaluate students' performance with anything other than in-class examinations. At the time of this writing, online examinations where students take the examination at home or in a living group have the limitation that you can never be sure who is taking the remote exam. Passwords provide no assistance—there is nothing to prevent an enrolled student from having illicit helpers at his or her elbow.

If you have readers, recitation section leaders, graders, or laboratory assistants, there is a wide variety of instruments you can use to assist in your evaluation, such as term papers, lab reports, field work, and so on. As most of them will actually be used in a small-class (section) context, your role is primarily to provide guidance to the assistants, and some sort of standardization. You don't want to have to deal with student complaints that one assistant's quizzes are much more difficult than another's.

I have laboratories with my big courses, and I like to provide a balance between allowing the lab assistants some leeway with their assignments, to permit a bit of creative teaching, and providing standardization to reduce student complaints. In a four-credit course with three lectures and a lab, I might set the evaluation program up with 400 points possible, 100 of which are to be distributed in the lab sections. At the first assistants' meeting, I'll give them some guidelines—maybe 25 points for a term paper, 30 for lab reports, the balance in quizzes. I then tell them to decide among themselves exactly how they want to distribute the points, but all of them have to agree on the number, and I have veto power—which I've never had to use. They are free to make up their own quizzes, but they have to show their quiz to at least two other assistants before they give it to their own class. This kind of peer assistance produces a remarkable uniformity in difficulty of assignments, saving me from having to impose an external standardization.

Homework

Any kind of assignment that students do at home adds to their educational experience. Unfortunately, if you evaluate this homework for a grade, you have no assurance (unless your college has an honor code) that the student in fact did the work.

There are a variety of ways of dealing with this, none 100% satisfactory. You can have the work count very little, so even if a student doesn't do the work, or plagiarizes, there is little consequence. The downside is that, knowing this, many students then tend to expend little effort.

Cheating

Cheating is probably the most unpleasant aspect of teaching. In large first-year classes, a certain fraction of students can be counted on to seize the opportunity to cheat. There is much you can do to reduce cheating, but it is almost impossible to eliminate it entirely without creating a police state environment in the class. You must also be extremely careful in both establishing your cheating policies, and enforcing them, because there can be serious legal consequences for both you and your institution if you falsely accuse a student of cheating and he or she can establish that the charge was groundless.

The first step in cheating reduction is to state your position on the matter in an unambiguous way on the first day of class. Because cheating is so common on my campus I spend a fair amount of time explaining why cheating is viewed by the academy as a crime, and treated accordingly. After many years of glassy-eyed responses to evocations of academic integrity, I stumbled onto a way of explaining things to them in terms that are relevant to their situation.

Because many of my students sooner or later will be competing with other people for jobs and professional schools, and admission to those desiderata depends on grades, I explain that a person who gets an illicit high grade through cheating is literally cheating everyone else out of a job, or a place in med school. Even though the cheater might not have lifted answers off a "victim's" paper during an examination, by getting a higher grade than he or she was entitled to, the cheater has diminished the value of the noncheater's grade. Therefore cheaters really do hurt students who don't cheat. A few sports metaphors make the explanation crystal clear. For example, what would be the value of an Olympic gold medal if the first three finishers in an event all got identical gold medals and they were awarded alphabetically on the podium? What would be the value of an Olympic gold medal if *everyone* who competed got one? That's how much an A would be worth if more people get them than deserve the distinction.

The second thing you need to do, and you must do this before the semester begins, is decide exactly what you will do if you catch a cheater. Give them a warning? Give them a zero? Turn them in to the college? My college's regulations insist that all cheating cases be forwarded to the dean, but this rule is more honored in the breach than the observance because 1) official cheating cases are a pain in the tail for instructors, and 2) if the instructor handles the situation locally, a much more appropriate and timely response is possible.

Whatever you decide your policy will be, the critical thing for your future peace of mind is to ensure that students know that you will do what you say you will do. If you are perceived as a paper tiger who issues direful threats but then slaps the wrist, you can look forward to many more cheating cases in the future. Once having established your policy, and following the principle that it is better to deter than to detect, you can then set in place some techniques to reduce the probability of successful cheating.

Cheating on Papers

For a major piece of work, such as a semester paper, there is an effective means of dealing with plagiarism, but it is not effort-free for the instructor. In a large class, anything like a semester paper almost has to be graded by section leaders or assistants. It is impossible to read 300–400 term papers of 10 pages apiece in a reasonable time period, but assistants can be told to use the same procedures you would use were the class smaller.

To minimize plagiarism on such assignments, the students are told that in addition to turning in their written paper, they must also "orally defend" it. What this means is that they must schedule a brief appointment—three minutes is all that's necessary—with the assistant who graded their paper, after all the papers have been graded. At this appointment all they have to do is define every word they used in their own paper and be able to explain, in simple English, any concept they discuss. If they are unable to do this, with their paper and notes in hand, the presumption is that they didn't do the work. Their score, whatever it had been, then turns to zero. They are told that even a terrible, failing paper that they wrote themselves will earn them a few points, but a plagiarized paper will earn them nothing.

The first time I tried this, 40% of the class got zeros. Word quickly spread, and by next semester, although the average quality of papers submitted had plummeted, the number of people who failed their defenses had gone almost to zero. I'm sure that some students may take a plagiarized paper and then bone up on it, but the effort required to do that would be almost as much, if not more, than would be expended on an original paper.

For the assistants, it means extra time above and beyond that required to correct the papers, but I usually schedule the paper defenses in lieu of a regular scheduled activity, for example a lab session, so it comes out in the wash.

Cheating on Exams

On exam day, if possible, scramble the students as they come into the auditorium. Don't allow them to sit in their customary seats. This will tend to break up any prearranged conspiracies.

When you prepare your examination on the computer, make two or three forms. This can be easily done by taking the first question or two on the original and putting them at the end, then renumbering. Repeat the process for a third form. This produces three forms with the same questions, but a student looking over a neighbor's answer sheet will copy down the wrong answers. Some of the canned question bank programs from publishers will automatically produce scrambled exams. If you want the students to know there are several forms, print them on different colored paper. If you would prefer to give students with wandering eyes an unpleasant surprise, print all the forms on the same colored paper and identify the forms by a subtle code on the answer sheet, which lies on top of the question sheets.

The advent of text messaging essentially means that every student now has a way of clandestinely contacting somebody out of class during an exam. In my subject (biology) I deal with this problem by acknowledging *force majeure*. For mid-semester exams, I allow the students to bring in a single page "cheat sheet" that must be handwritten (not copied) but can contain anything the student wants on both sides of the paper. Students will spend endless hours preparing their cheat sheets, and it is an enormously valuable study aid, because they have to actually think about what they should put on the sheets—the main value is in the preparation, rather than the possession. I make sure there are sufficient complex questions that texting students would simply run out of time, if they were dependent on a collaborator to look up information.

Internet Plagiarism

The World Wide Web has created rich new opportunities for students to plagiarize turned-in work with minimal effort. With the click of a mouse and a credit card number, students can buy prewritten term papers on almost *any* topic, or for a relatively modest extra fee can commission a paper on any topic. There are some altruistic web sites that have catalogs of term papers for impoverished plagiarists who cannot afford even the nominal fee charged by the commercial sites.

To acquaint yourself with the problem, I suggest you mentally convert yourself into a plagiarist and see what's available. For starters, take a look at the following commercial paper mills: *Evil House of Cheat (Cheathouse), Research Papers, A1 Termpaper*, and *Genius Papers*. Then, for free papers, my favorites are *School Sucks* and *Other People's Papers*. What you will find in most cases is a disclaimer ("These papers are to be used for research material only, and are not to be turned in as your own work"—yeah, right), a price (where appropriate), some outrageous claims about the quality of the papers, a search engine of some sort, and a teaser paragraph or two from the paper of interest. *School Sucks,* on its free "homework" page, makes the interesting argument that students aren't really cheating when they download homework from the site because the quality of homework that students upload is so abysmal that only an imbecile would try to submit it as his or her own work.

When I have pulled papers in my own area off the free sites, I have found them to be wildly varied in quality. Were I grading them, the average would be C, not the A quality claimed by the commercial sites. Nevertheless, for an otherwise failing student, a C on a major paper, for an investment of about 10 seconds of time and 10 sheets of inkjet paper, isn't such a bad deal.

How do you protect your honest students against this? As Giulio Douhet noted, "Every development or improvement in firearms favors the defensive." If it is easy for students to find prewritten papers on your topic, it is easy for you to find the same paper. Look at the most popular term paper sites first. If you feel lucky, pull out a sentence with an unusual construction or unusual vocabulary, put it in quotes, and enter it in a good search engine like Google or AltaVista. If the student's source was an article on the Internet (rather than a commercial paper), it should pop right out at you.

There are a couple of commercial sites that provide a plagiarism detection service through text analysis (for a fee.) You can find them in a search engine under "plagiarism detection." I hesitate to recommend them, not because they aren't effective, but because I take umbrage at having to fork over my own money to detect the bad guys. I would rather put the Fear into potential plagiarizers before they even reach for their mice.

If you have a small class, it is fairly easy to run all of your moderately to mildly suspicious papers through such scrutiny, but in a large class, you (and your assistants) will have to do some quick nonelectronic scanning first. There are a couple of clues that should ring alarm bells. If the paper is very erratic in style, with carefully phrased technical paragraphs separated by barely literate bridge paragraphs, that suggests a cut-and-paste job. If the whole paper is consistently good, but the student's previous work has been marginal or below, it *could* be a near-miracle of fast learning, but an alternative explanation is more likely. If the topic of the paper is way off the assigned topic, especially if the assigned topic is fairly specialized, flags should go up.

To reduce students' temptation to use the Internet for plagiarism, it doesn't do any harm to let them know when they get their assignments that you know about Internet plagiarism, how it works, and how easy it is for you to catch it. Preferably you will let them know this in writing.

The more general the topic you give them, the easier it will be for them to find a suitable plagiarizable match. To allow them to come up with their own topics is a wonderful way to encourage students to write about what they have an interest in, but it is also almost an invitation to steal for students who are ethically challenged.

After the Test Is Over

Once you have established how you will evaluate your students' knowledge, for most instructors the next task will be developing a grading scheme. In the next chapter, you'll see that there is a wide variety of grading plans, but each of them can be adjusted to produce about the same final result.

8

GRADING

And to the C students, I say you, too, can become president.
—George W. Bush, Yale University commencement

There is little to no national grading standardization in colleges and universities. Although there is universal agreement that an A grade is probably better than a C, one college's A may be a mark of rare academic distinction, while another's may simply indicate that a student has a pleasing personality and turned in her work on time. A Google search for "college grading standards" revealed every variety of policy. For example, Tacoma Community College's English department lists the detailed and specific criteria that student work must demonstrate to receive a particular letter grade. The web site of the Undergraduate Study Committee of Berkeley's Department of Electrical Engineering and Computer Science doesn't address the question of criteria to be used to award grades, but suggests a "typical" class average for a lower division course might be 2.7 (out of 4). This average might be achieved by a suggested distribution of 17% As, 50% Bs, 20% Cs, 10% Ds, and 3% Fs. The same site also notes, "In some courses, the assigned grades show wide fluctuation from section to section and/or semester, depending on who teaches the section. Furthermore, over the last 10 years, the lower and upper division course averages have inflated considerably." My university's grading definitions in its faculty manual declined in specificity over the years:

1980	2001
A: Superior	A: Superior
B: Good, above average but not superior	B: Good
C: Average	C: Fair
D: Low grade, below average, passing	D: Low grade, passing
F: Failure	F: Failure

While in 1980 an average score would earn a student a C, in 2001 an average score could be subjectively interpreted by an instructor to be "good," thus yielding a B, and who could say nay? The seeds for "grade inflation" were thereby planted.

A few colleges issue a percentage equivalent definition for grades. For example, 90%–100% means A, 80%–89% means B, and so forth. This appears to be both a tool for standardization and an accurate representation of performance, but left unasked is the question, "Ninety percent *of what?*" Professor Jones might hold her students responsible for, say, 200 units of information. Ninety percent of that is 180 units of information. Professor Smith might hold her students responsible for 300 units of information. Eighty percent of that is 240 units of information. A performance that would produce an off-the-charts A in Professor A's class would yield a squeaker B in Professor B's class, yet to the outside world, both professors would seem to be using the same grading criteria. This hidden uncertainty allows a college or instructor to claim that students are being held to a high standard (i.e., "You need to have a 75% to pass this course!") while actually allowing the student to sail through with a minimal demonstration of knowledge. The opposite, of course, can also be true—a course can appear to be deceptively easy if a low percentage score is required for a given letter grade but the students are expected to master huge amounts of information.

A handful of colleges have just pass-fail grading, and the abovementioned few have instructors report grades as a percentage, but most colleges have a categorized letter grade (A, B, C, D, F) system. Some systems are more finely divided (A, A–, B+, etc.) than others. However, the intrinsic difficulty with any categorization system is that it attempts to take what is essentially a continuum, student performance, and divide it into arbitrary segments where there is no real "natural" division between categories. Because the placement of students into these categories is so important to students' lives, there is a tendency of colleges to pretend that the divisions between grade categories are not as arbitrary as they actually are. Scholarships, admission to graduate or professional school, and jobs may all depend on a couple of tenths of a grade point difference between students. Colleges do not like to say, "A student with a 2.75 average *may* be a better scholar than one with a 2.53, but luck has a lot to do with it—the 2.53 student may just have had the misfortune of ending up in a lot of classes with professors who had a different grading system than did the student with the 2.75."

If you are new to the grading process, a faculty handbook or university manual might be a place to start. Before you develop your own system for assigning students to categories, it is not a bad idea to see if your college provides any guidelines. Your institution may deal with the issue in more concrete fashion than mine. Conversation with colleagues, if they are willing to talk about it, is not a bad idea, either. If you are new to a long-established big course, it is very important to know what the grading practices have been in the past because students will tend to expect them to be the same when you take over.

As you've seen, a percentage system (A = 90–100, B = 80–89, etc.) gives a deceptive appearance of precision. A system that is less precise on the face of it, but more accurate in practice, relies on a series of descriptive qualifications that you can use to determine in which grade box a student should be placed. For example, a professor might define his or her grade categories as follows:

1. To earn a D (pass) in this course, a student must demonstrate a satisfactory knowledge of the vocabulary of the subject and show that he or she has, at a minimum, performed all the reading assignments. He or she should not have more than 10% unexcused absences.

2. To earn a C in this course, in addition to the above, a student will demonstrate that he or she can solve simple problems in the subject and has a basic grasp of the general principles covered in the lecture and reading assignments. All assignments shall be performed on time.

3. To earn a B in this course, in addition to the above, the student will consistently solve more difficult problems and show, by his or her questions and participation in class discussion, that he or she is fully familiar with the principles covered in assignments. The student's writing ability, as shown in term papers, will be good and without major flaws in grammar, punctuation, and syntax.

4. To earn an A in this course, in addition to the above, the student will be able to solve difficult and complex problems. His or her written assignments will be imaginative and well thought out and he or she will demonstrate a high degree of creativity and participation in the laboratory or recitation section.

With this description of the qualities needed to earn a particular grade, assignments can then be devised to make sure that students have an opportunity to demonstrate these qualities. Obviously, if grading is based 100% on multiple-choice examinations that require memorization of facts as the only skill to be demonstrated, the category descriptions are meaningless.

Many of the words or phrases used in the descriptions above are subjective—for example, "major flaws," "basic grasp of general principles." Juries are faced with the same subjectivity when they are asked to determine guilt "to a certainty beyond reasonable doubt." What is "reasonable"?

Whenever there are categories that do not have natural, clearly defined boundaries, some injustice is bound to occur. A suspect guilty in the eyes of one jury might be found innocent by another, even when the juries are presented with the same evidence. Similarly, identical student performances can be legitimately assigned different grades by different instructors.

As an individual instructor, there is little you can do about this variation between instructors. Lacking tightly defined institutional standards for performance, one can only hope that a superior student will end up with a higher grade point than an average student, but Lady Luck has a hand in this determination. What you *can* do in your own class is make sure that your grading system is understandable, equitable, and internally consistent. For large classes, manageability is also an important consideration.

Categories of Categorization

There are only two major kinds of category grading systems used in colleges. The first is the *absolute* (or "criterion referenced," in educationalese) system, where the teacher assigns students to the various grade categories on the basis of their absolute performance. Thus, at the beginning of the semester, the teacher might say, "To earn an A in this course, by the end of the semester you must have a total percentage score that falls between 90% and 100%; to earn a B, your score must fall between 80% and 89%" and so on. Tradition and custom suggest the round numbers as the dividing points, but there is no real reason why a teacher couldn't make it 92%–100%, or 88%–100%.

There are two characteristics of this system that you need to be aware of. First, it is inherently noncompetitive; a student's final grade depends on his or her performance alone, not on relative position in the class. Cooperative behavior is easier to encourage in this system because helping a fellow student cannot jeopardize a student's own grade. Second, unless the instructor is fairly familiar with the capabilities of a class in relation to the difficulties of the assignments, it is *possible* in such a system to end up with no students receiving good grades (or more students with good grades than most people would consider reasonable). Finally, students have a known and fixed mark to shoot for—get that 90% and you have an A, no matter what the class average.

In this system, the fraction of the class that falls into each grade category is determined by an interaction between 1) the ability of the class, and 2) the difficulty of the assignments and evaluation instruments. Without some experience as to the match between students and difficulty, it is possible for an instructor's grade distributions to swing wildly from semester to semester until he or she develops a "feel" for the level of difficulty that will produce a desired distribution of grades.

If an instructor wants to use an absolute system because of the advantages it confers, yet still wishes to have a predictable and consistent fraction of the class fall in each category, he or she can do it by manipulating the cut lines between categories. There is nothing inherently sacred about the round numbers as cuts: 87%–100% for an A is as defendable as 90%–100%. Pushing the lines too far will raise eyebrows, however. If in your class the A bracket is 75%–100%, your explanations of the hellacious difficulty of your examinations may fall on deaf collegial ears.

If in your class you'd like to award the top 10% of the class As, the next 20% Bs, and so on yet still use an absolute standard, it is possible to do so by looking over several semesters' worth of records for your course.

If the characteristics of the class haven't changed over that time, and you haven't changed the difficulty of the assignments, you should be able to see a rough pattern emerging such that if you divided A from B at 88% and B from C at 77%, you would end up with your 10%–20% distribution. Make those your absolute dividing lines in subsequent semesters.

The other major grading system is the *relative* (or "norm-referenced") system. With this method, the instructor states, in advance, what fraction of the class will receive a certain grade, typically 10–20–40–20–10 (this assumes, of course, a normal distribution of scores). The great advantage of this system is that with no experience with the class at all, and regardless of the difficulty or ease of the assignments, the desired distribution of letter grades will be produced.

A disadvantage of the system is that with a poorly prepared class and a demanding teacher, it is entirely possible for a student to receive an A and only have a final percentage score of, say, 35%. A credibility problem is then created both for the student and instructor. How can a student have an A– (superior) grade, while knowing only 35% of the material? Conversely, with an extremely lenient instructor, a student might end up with a 95% and receive a C because half the class had better scores.

An advantage of a relative system is that if an outsider, say a potential employer, is trying to evaluate a student's performance and knows that a relative system was used, the outsider knows that a student who received an A is at the very top of the class. True, the student may be the best of a bad lot, but at least the student is at the top. In an absolute system with an easy instructor, 40% of the class might receive As, and there is no way of telling whether a student was at the top or in the middle of the class. Unfortunately for employers, professional schools, and the like, college transcripts rarely indicate the type of grading system used in a class, so this remains a theoretical advantage for those who must interpret a candidate's transcript. Some colleges are beginning to address this issue by posting class standings along with grades.

In large, lower division classes, it has traditionally been assumed that whatever the system, there will be a normal distribution of performances, and therefore grade distributions around C will be symmetrical—there will be about as many As as Fs. For a variety of reasons, this is no longer a safe assumption. Admission policies may cause a skewed or even bimodal distribution of performances. If performance distributions are skewed to the left—that is, toward the lower performing side of the class—many grading systems will produce an F category that has two to three times more students than the A category. From a statistical standpoint, such a distribution simply reflects reality, but in an era where student retention is important to an institution's budget, such a distribution is of concern not only to faculty but also to the administration.

Resolving this difficulty for an instructor is often more a matter of being attuned to campus politics than pedagogy. As you have seen, grades in a class are whatever an instructor chooses to make them. For some instructors an A is a mark of rare distinction. Others are more generous. If *your* grade distribution is markedly different from that of the colleagues in your department who teach similar courses at the same year level, you can be assured that there will be some administrative interest in your policies. The concept of academic freedom will prohibit administrative *intrusion* into your grading practices in most cases, but there are subtle ways of conveying disapproval. Students will rarely, if ever, complain if your grading is perceived to be too easy, but if it is significantly less generous than your counterparts' policies at a different institution, whose grads your students will have to compete with for grad school admissions, you may end up sabotaging your own students' chances. Lack of national grading standards and competition for jobs and professional school admittances have led to a marked inflation in college grades.

Close examination of the absolute and relative systems will show that with suitable manipulation both can produce essentially the same results. A relative system can produce a predictable cut line between letter grades, while preserving a predetermined number of students in each category, by manipulation of the difficulty of the assignments. An absolute system can produce a predictable number of students in each category by prior manipulation of the cut lines. In both cases, some experience with the class is necessary. For instructors new to teaching large classes, I usually recommend starting with a relative system to avoid disastrous grade distributions, then switching over to an absolute system because of its noncompetitive, predictable nature for students.

There are a few other grading systems that one can find in use. Instructors with class sizes on the small end of the large-class spectrum will sometimes draw a histogram of the students' total scores at the end of the semester, then look for "natural" breaks between clusters of grades to place the divisions between letter grades. These breaks tend not to be "natural" in the sense that they represent groupings of students whose abilities are more similar to one another's than they are to students' abilities in the other groups. Rather, they are simply the statistical clumping that is the result of a relatively small class size. The only real advantage of this system is that it tends to reduce complaints from students who missed the next higher grade by one point. The disadvantage lies mostly on the student side—there is no concrete performance target for a student to aim for in his or her quest for a specific grade.

Some instructors who are comfortable with statistics use grading systems based on statistical principles. The most common starts with the assumption that student scores are normally distributed (the bell-shaped curve). The class mean, or average, is then calculated, then the standard deviation, which is a measure of the scatter of values around the mean. Some multiple of the standard deviation is then used to set the boundaries of the grades. For example, if a multiple of 1.3 times the standard deviation is used to set the lower boundary of A grades, and 1.0 times the standard deviation to set each lower grade boundary, the result will be 7% As, 24% Bs, 38% Cs, 24% Ds, and 7% Fs. If there is *not* a normal distribution, for example if it is skewed or bimodal, then this method loses the mathematical underpinnings of its use.

Such a system has the advantage of looking "scientific" and hence generates few student complaints. However, at its heart, it is just as arbitrary as any other method. Why not use 1.2, or .9, as the multiple to set the boundaries in order to get the grade distribution you feel comfortable with? No reason at all.

Non-Normal Distributions

Large classes *should* display a normal distribution of performance, with relatively small (and equal) numbers of students at the extremes, with the bulk of the class centered around the class average. However, it is becoming increasingly common at the kinds of colleges that have large classes to see a flattened distribution, with more students at the extremes than one would expect, or skewed (typically toward the low end) or even bimodal distributions with peaks at the extremes, and a flat spot in the center. These situations can produce great difficulties for instructors.

With a class that has a normal distribution, you can't go far astray by tailoring the level of your presentation toward the middle of the class. The greatest number of students are in this category, and the relatively small number of extremes aren't that far from the middle. However, with the worst-case bimodal distribution, there are very few students in the middle, and if you aim at either of the extremes, the other extreme is going to be either terminally bored or impossibly confused.

I'm not aware of any truly satisfactory ways of dealing with this. When it has happened in my big classes, I've tried a few techniques that have had some success, but all of them require an enormous amount of time.

To give me early warning of what the situation is going to be, I schedule a "mini-exam," only two and a half weeks into the semester. This is really just a quiz, but it has the trappings of an examination—same format, same type of questions, and so forth. It is not for "practice": It counts toward the grade, but not much, so if a student blows it, no real harm is done. The only difference between it and a regular examination is that it has only 10 questions and is based on a couple of chapters. Based on the experience of a couple of years, I can then make some predictions about what the distribution of scores will be on the first regular examination and prepare the difficulty level accordingly.

After the first full examination, those students who fail are told that they *must* come in to see me for a personal office visit and study consultation. The students are told to come prepared to answer three questions: 1) Why do *you* (the student) think you failed the examination? 2) What specific steps do *you* propose to take to make sure it doesn't happen again? 3) What can *I* (the instructor) do to help you? This discussion is very illuminating because students often are clueless about the reasons for their failure—the same amount and kind of study they are currently doing brought them As in high school. I spend 5–10 minutes with each one. In my larger classes, I might have to see more than 125 students in a two-week period, leaving little time for anything else. Does it help? In the first semester after I started doing it, my end-of-semester failure rate dropped by one-third and that number has somewhat improved in subsequent semesters—all without lowering grading standards. Is this an appropriate use of a senior professor's time at a research university? As I have pointed out to my administrator colleagues, if this procedure keeps just five students in school, who would otherwise have flunked out, dropped out, or transferred, I have saved the university in that one semester more money than I would have generated in research overhead for the whole year in my field. Although the students pick up some study tips, I have the feeling that the real reason the technique works is that the students have the feeling that even though it is a big class, someone actually *cares* whether they do well.

For the better students in class, I have a standing offer that if they're bored with the regular assignments and can demonstrate to me that they already have a mastery of the subject, I'll work with them on a custom package of readings, consultations, lab work, or whatever they want so that they can learn something new—all without a grade penalty. I have the occasional student take me up on it, but what I hear from these students when I run into them again in upper division courses is that they would rather take an easy, no-effort A and spend the liberated time on their more challenging courses or outside activities. As a result, I have a fairly easy conscience about neglecting the top group and spending disproportionately more time with the ones hanging on by their fingernails.

Special Considerations

Makeups
There are always students who miss assignments and examinations, sometimes for good cause, and you will need to establish a consistent policy about makeup work before the semester begins. Some instructors don't have a makeup policy—if a student misses an exam, that's his or her problem. If you are going to permit makeup work, however, there are several alternatives. If you have a number of roughly equal-weight assignments, say three one-hour exams or weekly quizzes, you can allow students to automatically drop their lowest score and the percentage will

be calculated on the revised total (you need to realize that this artificially raises the class average and may have an impact on your distribution of letter grades). If a student misses an exam, that becomes his or her de facto lowest score and is dropped automatically—you don't need to bother with excuses or doctor's notes. However, what do you do if a student misses a *second* assignment?

You can always do nothing. Into each life a little rain must fall. If you are sympathetic to the student's case, you don't want to drop a second exam and calculate a percentage on the balance of available points because that might actually give the student an *advantage* by missing the assignment. On the other hand, if the student has satisfactorily completed a fair number of other, similar assignments, you can prorate the missed assignment—calculate the average score, say 75%, on completed assignments, and figure that the student *would have done* about as well on the missed assignment as on the completed ones. You therefore give the student the average percentage on the missed assignment. If it were a missed 10-point quiz, you'd give the student 7.5 points. If the missed assignment is unique, say a term paper or a single mid-semester examination, then it is difficult to impossible to apply this technique.

I go about handling makeups in a slightly different way. If students miss an exam, I simply let them take a makeup examination—but it is always in essay format. Clearly, they can't be given the same multiple-choice examination that all the other students took because the answers are all over the campus five minutes after the examination is over. At the same time, I don't want to make up a 40-question multiple-choice examination for just one student. Instead, all the student has to do is make an appointment with me anytime between the end of the missed examination and the date of the next examination and take the makeup at a time of mutual convenience. I don't have to be a cop checking on the authenticity of their excuse with this method, although obviously if the student has spent an enormous amount of time developing a creative excuse to con me into allowing him or her to take a makeup, I would be a cad indeed if I didn't listen to it, stroke my chin, sympathize about the tragic loss of their cousin in the awful accident, and then allow them to take the makeup. In my case, once the word got around that it was easy to get a makeup, but the makeup was an essay, there was an amazing drop in the number of grandmothers who unexpectedly passed away during the semester.

Borderlines

If your class is big enough, there will be substantial numbers of students who are one point away from the next higher grade by the end of the semester. You may, with perfect justification, express to your students at the beginning of the semester the idea that such is the nature of life, close doesn't count, 89.9999 is a B+, and that's the way it is.

On the other hand, especially in first-year courses, it is quite common for students to start badly because they have "freshmanitis," get with the program, and end up doing quite well. However, because of their bad early performance, an A performance on the final might be pulled down to a B− for the semester, once the earlier scores are factored in. You may wish to recognize this improvement in an individual student by departing slightly from the fixed relationship between numerical score (or percentage) and letter grade. Unless you handle this carefully you will open yourself up to an endless stream of students who heard about their lucky compatriots and will beseech you with plea bargaining requests after the semester is over.

I handle this by incorporating into the printed course rules two rare exceptions to the usual rule that percentage score equals letter grade. The first exception is where I have personal knowledge that a student who had received otherwise good scores had blown an examination through circumstances beyond his or her control, for example having gotten news of a family death just before an examination. If the throw-out-the-worst-exam system were used, this exception would not be necessary. It would seem that students would abuse this bit of largesse, but I have not found it to be the case in practice.

The second exception is where a student is a point below the next higher grade, and the final examination is "substantially" better than his or her average scores. In this case, I'll consider a boost to the next higher grade. *Substantial* is a subjective term, of course, and allows me a little executive leeway.

In a class of 300, perhaps a half-dozen students will meet the qualifications. Adopting this system means that two students could have identical final scores but different final letter grades, but I've not had any squawks from students about this—they seem to understand that the system recognizes improvement and thus can only be to their advantage.

Multiple-Section Grading

There are two cases where several parties might be involved in the grading process. In the first, there is a lecturer who supervises a number of graduate students teaching recitation or laboratory sections who feed recitation or lab scores to the course instructor. In the second, there might be several lecturers teaching different lecture sections of the same course simultaneously, or several instructors sequentially lecturing to the same group of students, a situation sometimes called "team teaching," although there may be precious little teamwork involved.

The first case presents few problems besides administrative and managerial difficulties. Grades can be normalized between sections as described in Chapter 4, and the assistants are really assistants, whose job is to help you. The administrative structure is basically hierarchical, and you are the Boss.

When multiple faculty are involved in a single course, the situation is more delicate. Faculty members tend to have strong and diverse opinions about testing and grading, but only one grade per student can be turned in at the end of the semester.

Like-minded faculty might get together and decide, "Let's do a course on XY! I can do the X lectures, you do the Ys, we'll both sit in on each other's lectures, and we can write the exams together. After all these years talking with you, we have similar ideas on how students should be graded, and it'll be a ball!" And it would be. However, a more typical multiple-instructor arrangement is something cobbled together by a department chair who has instructors who need bits and pieces of teaching credits to make up their teaching load. The participants may loathe each other after years of departmental squabbling and have diametrically opposite views on teaching, testing, and grading.

Differences in lecture styles present little difficulty—students always have mixed reactions to any one style, and a student who strongly dislikes the first lecturer in a series may love the second, while his or her seatmate has just the opposite reaction. The stickiness arises not from the lecture, but in grading.

Some departments may have multiple lecturers, but all teach from a standardized syllabus, and their students take common examinations prepared as a result of negotiations between the lecturers. Such an arrangement can have a stifling effect on lecturer creativity but eliminates differences in grade performance between sections caused by differences of opinion between the participants about grading practice. However, it also tends to increase the practice of "teaching to the test." Another unwelcome side effect is that if an instructor finds that his or her lecture section is having a particularly hard time dealing with a concept, it is difficult for that instructor to devote extra time to the subject without having the class fall behind the syllabus and possibly be at risk on the next examination.

Where there are multiple lecturers, each of whom makes up his or her own lecture examinations, some of these problems are addressed, but it is unlikely that randomly selected lecturers will have the same grading theory, so the distribution of grades between the sections can differ, sometimes widely.

Students readily compare notes, and it is likely that the "tougher" instructor will draw more student complaints about grading than if the policies were the same, but he or she was the sole lecturer. What happens after that depends on too many factors to be able to make a general prediction. First-year students are more affected by their perceptions of an instructor's grading practices than advanced students, and if students have a choice between an "easy" instructor and a "hard" one for the same course, all other things being equal there will be a tendency to gravitate toward the easier one's sections. If tenure and promotion decisions at an institution are strongly influenced by student evaluations, an untenured instructor who finds that his or her standards are markedly higher than a co-teacher in a course may have a strong personal disincentive to continue with that practice.

Squawks

No matter how well thought out your grading procedure, there will be complaints about it. That's just human nature. Students are unlikely to come to you and say, "You gave me a B+ and I only deserved a C+. Would you change it, please?" The reverse request can be expected. By their nature, complaints about grades must be handled individually, but you will want to remember that resolving complaints in big courses is very much like case law in the legal world—once a precedent has been established, it is very difficult to deny the next plaintiff equal relief. The student communication network is unbelievably efficient, and once it is known that a certain approach has been successful with you there will be others to follow.

Unless you *like* the idea of dealing with a parade of students outside your door when the final grades are posted, your best grading policy is one that is simple, clear, unambiguous, and delivered in writing at the beginning of the semester. This policy should not be so rigid that you cannot accommodate the occasional legitimate squawk, but should be tight enough to prevent endless lines of supplicants in the future.

Many colleges have formal procedures in place for students to object to what they consider "unfair" grades. Typically a student will go to the professor first, then the department chair, then the dean and/or some kind of campus judicial board set up to handle grading disputes, and finally a campus ombudsman, if there is one. In recent years, parents often run interference for their kids, adding a new and delicate dimension to the issue. When I was department chair, I used to hate to get involved in these matters. More often than not, the student would have a legitimate grouse because the grading instructions in the course were vague, contradictory, or not administered in an evenhanded way. "Academic freedom," however, said that I couldn't butt in (nor could the dean) if the instructor was intransigent, and it would be up to me to explain to the student that, yes, they did have a point, but no, there wasn't anything I could do about it. Needless to say, my feelings toward the faculty member who had put me in this position were not warm.

According to our ombudsman, the vast majority of disputed grade cases that make it to the office involve not judgment calls about, say, how a paper should have been graded, but unclear grading policies that allowed some degree of interpretation on the student's part. Naturally, when given this opportunity, students will interpret things in their favor and be unpleasantly surprised when, after the fact, the instructor doesn't allow that view.

Students rarely win disputed grade cases, but they can involve an outrageous amount of faculty time (and emotional stress), and as a large-class instructor, you are far more likely to face them than you would in a small class. Again, the very best way to avoid them is to have a clear, specific, written grading policy that is issued to the students on the first day of class and allows very little wiggle room in its interpretation.

Students will remember the grade you issue to them long after they have forgotten most of the facts that you presented. Like it or not, grades can have a profound effect on your students' lives, so the humane, professional teacher will spend considerable attention and effort in making sure that the grading system is as equitable, valid, and reliable as possible.

9

The Seasons of a Class

To every thing there is a season, and a time to every purpose under the heaven.
—Ecclesiastes 3:1

Every class has a rhythm and a flow. Fall semester courses are different than spring ones. Students' enthusiasms rise and fall as they transition from scared newbies on the first day of class to sadder-but-wiser veterans by the end of the semester. By recognizing that some things just won't work in a large class until new students have a few weeks under their belts, you can save yourself and them a lot of frustration and wasted time.

Some instructors, aware of all the "content" they must cover during the term, like to get right to it and immediately start on the meat of the course in the first lecture of the semester. They are then surprised when it appears from the results of the first examination that virtually no students went to class that first day. In fall semester freshman courses, students are so occupied with appearing cool, while actually feeling intimidated, that they have the attention span of a Siamese cat (actually, because I own a couple of Siamese cats, I know that statement is insulting to Siamese). On the first day of a large, sophomore-level course, there will be a sufficient undercurrent of jabber as friends discuss what went on over the break or summer that the instructor's voice will need an extra 10 decibels out of the loudspeakers. So the first day is pretty much of a washout for content. However, as described in Chapter 2, it is marvelous for setting the tone, mood, and flavor of the course.

As the semester wears on for first-year students, they gain proficiency in study skills and learn that college really is different from high school. The middle third of the course is probably the most productive for both them and you. They have pretty much adapted to college life and are optimistic about the future. This means you can pick up the pace and go into more detail and complexity than you could at the beginning of the semester.

However, in the final third of the course several factors dictate that you slow down a bit. For some students, fear returns as they realize that it is going to be difficult to impossible to catch up. A semester of late-night partying and/or studying begins to catch up to them, and simple fatigue enters the picture. For many of them, end-of-semester projects come due in other courses and routine reading and studying have to take a backseat. For this reason, I usually distribute my reading assignments unevenly during the semester. After the first week or two of the semester, when they have had a chance to settle in, I hit them hard with readings to capitalize on early-semester energy, especially in fall courses. The reading load tapers off during the semester, and in the final two or three weeks their weekly reading assignment is half what it was at the beginning of the semester. This reading reduction has the added advantage of allowing those students who want to begin an end-of-semester review sufficient time to do it.

When I teach the same first-year course in both fall and spring, I notice some differences. In the spring you have a noticeably more mature group of students who have gotten over the first-semester trauma. Unfortunately, if you teach a major's course, you will also have a fairly substantial chunk of the students who failed the course in first semester. These students tend to be less than enthusiastic (for obvious reasons) about the course, but I try to say a few words to them collectively during the first lecture. They have an admittedly tough row to hoe because they've heard all your jokes, the book isn't going to be any more interesting the second time around, and the stakes are likely to be higher—they may be on academic probation. I tell them that hard as it will be to do, they have to pretend that they've never taken the course before. Their temptation will be to neither attend lectures nor read the chapters. After all, they supposedly had *already* read the chapters. I point out to them that although they may have *read* the chapters, if they had *understood* the chapters, they wouldn't be sitting where they are today. About a third of my "alumni" fail the class the second time also.

Student Evaluations of Teaching

Student evaluations of teaching, although they first started in the 1920s, really began to proliferate in the 1960s and are now widespread on college campuses. In the 1960s, they were a spinoff of the student movement and were intended as a guide to help students avoid dreadful instructors. The information was collected informally by students and distributed usually as a supplement to the student newspaper. An instructor who was in disfavor with the editors might find himself looking at something like these gems I recall from my Berkeley undergraduate days. "Professor Gold's monotone could be used by the Bureau of Standards. It has been reported that Professor Green is actually dead. This cannot be confirmed because no one can tell the difference between the lectures Professor Green gives now versus those he might give if he were dead."

College administrations and instructors soon co-opted these evaluations and began using them for different purposes—assisting administrators in promotion and tenure decisions, and only secondarily using the information gathered to help instructors improve their teaching. In the former case, suddenly, what had been merely a potentially embarrassing annoyance now became a career-influencing event.

There have been more than 2,000 published papers on the reliability and validity of student evaluations of teaching. The results of these studies are both equivocal and controversial. However, for your purposes, if promotion, tenure, or retention hinge on student evaluations at your institution, *it doesn't matter whether they are reliable or valid,* as long as the person or body deciding your fate believes they are.

Asking questions of students about your teaching can indeed be a valuable resource to help you improve your teaching. However, the questions an administrator might use on a student evaluation of teaching (SET) form to help rank your performance against a colleague or a standard often have little utility in helping you refine your teaching. For example, one of the agree-disagree statements used on the administrative SET form on my campus is, "Has an effective style of presentation." Suppose your students give you a very bad rating on this question. That tells your dean that your style of presentation is less effective than

Professor X's, but it doesn't give you a clue about *why* your style is ineffective. Do you have a world-class collection of annoying gestures and speech mannerisms? Do you never use words of less than eight syllables? Another statement is, "Treats students as mature individuals." What is the correct interpretation of a negative response to this question if you have a lot of students who are 17 and spectacularly immature? Is treating immature students as mature adults a good thing or a bad thing?

This conundrum may produce a problem for you. At most colleges that use an SET, it is mandated by the administration (or in some cases, by a body like a faculty senate). So you don't really have a choice about whether to give the administration's SET. The results may be of negligible value to you if you want to improve your teaching, although they may help you to keep your job.

The only real solution is to give the students *another* SET, one custom tailored to your course, whose purpose is not really evaluation but generation of information. You want to word the questions in such a way that an interpretation of the answer is clear and specific to your course. For example, "How many help sessions did you go to this semester? 0–1__; 2–3__; 4 or more___" is unambiguous. If your campus has an instructional or faculty development program, the folks there can be very helpful in designing a useful form. Unfortunately, your questionnaire is *in addition* to the college's, and I have found that once past their first semester many students tend to be cynics about the impact their opinions on a college SET will have on changing teachers' behavior, and they tend to blow all SETs off. I therefore explain that *my* questionnaire will be read carefully and taken seriously. I also leave a lot of room for write-in opinions. Needless to say, some students who might not be doing too well in the course may regard this as a golden opportunity for payback, so some of the write-ins may well include some colorful language and imaginative suggestions about what you can do to yourself and your anatomy.

So, you will administer your own SET to give you concrete suggestions to improve your teaching, but in the interest of maximizing the probability that you will return for another semester of teaching, how do you maximize your ratings on the college's SET? The educational literature does not offer any clear suggestions—you can find well-done papers that both support and argue against the relationship between lenient grading and good SETs, for example. So, what I will pass on to you is strictly anecdotal—take it for what it's worth. I'll also add that these comments do not necessarily apply to small and/or upper division classes with more mature students.

In looking at my own, and colleague's SETs, there seems to be a fairly strong association between students' perceptions of the *personality* of the instructor and ratings. Friendly, easygoing, approachable, and reasonable seem to be the money qualities. In other words—"cool!" Demanding, strict, brilliant, and adhering to high standards do not seem to be generally attractive qualities to lower division students. The *perception* of grading policies appears to have more impact than actual policies. For this reason, in the window of time that you will have to administer your college SET, you might consider administering the SET halfway between the last exam and the next one, so grades will not be in the forefront of students' minds while they are assessing your teaching qualities. Students often have short memories. Suppose you *are* normally demanding, have high expectations, and offer challenging lectures that dictate strict attention. If you make the lecture immediately before you hand out the SET forms a bit more relaxed, and dare it be said, "fun," you might be pleasantly surprised by the outcome.

Classroom Research

You learned about assessment—activities designed to give you day-to-day information on how your class is doing—in Chapter 7. By expanding on these activities and formalizing them a bit you are now doing educational research and may get a bit of extra mileage out of your teaching: some publications.

There are several well-respected refereed journals that publish articles on educational research in undergraduate education, among them the *Journal on Excellence in College Teaching, New Directions for Higher Education, College Teaching,* and *Journal of Research in College Teaching.* There are also more specialized journals, such as *Teaching Sociology, Journal of College Science Teaching, Science Education,* and *American Biology Teacher.* A number of professional societies, for example the American Chemical

Society and American Physical Society, have publications that deal with college teaching, much of it in a large-class context.

These journals not only can be a source of valuable tips for you, but can also be a venue for publications that will pay you back a bit for the extra time you are taking away from your specialty research to improve your teaching. A publication counts for your curriculum vitae as long as it is refereed, and if you are going to be doing assessment activities anyway, just expand the activity a bit and now you have an extra publication. I won't kid you: In most institutions that have large classes, research in your specialty will always be important for promotion and tenure and you ignore it at your peril. However, research for a teaching journal provides a valuable service to the teaching community and can convert some of that time you're spending on good teaching into the coin of the realm in academia—publications.

Grants

Say the word *grant* and the first thing that comes into most academics' heads is "specialty research." However, times have changed and, in many fields, grants for the improvement of teaching are easier to get, and larger, than traditional research grants. In my research field, animal behavior, the typical acceptance rate for grant proposals at the National Science Foundation (NSF) is 8%–13%. On recent grant panels on which I have served at NSF in the Undergraduate Education directorate, acceptances have been running 30%–50%, although it is now somewhat lower. In my department in recent years, we have picked up hundreds of thousands of dollars to improve our large-class lecture halls and upgrade our laboratories through education grants.

By developing a bit of expertise in teaching, and doing some cross-disciplinary reading in education, you may well find that you can generate as much or more grant overhead through teaching-related activities as you can from discipline-related research. There are several large national foundations that sponsor higher education grants, in particular the Howard Hughes Medical Education Foundation and the Lilly Foundation. The federal Department of Education and the NSF are both sponsors of research in higher education.

Local foundations can often be tapped for grants to improve large-class teaching. One of the things such foundations look for is a body count: How many students will benefit if the grant is awarded? As a large-class teacher you have the numbers on your side.

The Last Lecture

When I was an undergraduate at Berkeley in the early 1960s there was a charming custom that the final lecture of the semester be something special. In fact, it was usually called "The Last Lecture." In this lecture the instructor would try to impart some wisdom to the class, in addition to the knowledge that had been dispensed during the semester. If the class wished to indicate their approval of the instructor's efforts during the past four months, they would reward him or her with a round of applause before they departed. As I recall, only a few classes were so bad that the class simply got up after The Last Lecture was over and left in silence. I cannot begin to imagine how devastating that must have felt.

In most classes The Last Lecture was about as memorable as the rest of the class had been—that is, not very. After a perfunctory but polite few claps of applause, the class and instructor would both go about their respective businesses. However, three of the teachers I had at Berkeley were so staggeringly good that they positively changed my life. I have spent the last 38 years as a college professor trying to figure out just what it was that made them so influential and whether I might be able to drink from the same bottle of magical elixir and have a similar effect on my classes.

Two of the three taught small classes and I think much of their magic depended on us being able to see them do, with staggering proficiency, the thing they taught about. The third, however, taught a huge class. I was one of more than 400 students in Richard Eakin's embryology course. It might be instructive to pass on to you what I think made him such a marvelous large-class instructor.

The lectures themselves were technically perfect. Start on time, finish on time, beginning-middle-end, balance between principles and examples—the very model of what a well-constructed lecture should be. His voice was beautifully modulated and reached to the back rows. (I later found out that he had been very active in drama as an undergraduate.)

However, perfect lectures alone do not a great lecturer make. Although he was an internationally known researcher who was one of the jewels in Berkeley's crown, he let us know that teaching was both his greatest joy and privilege. We believed him. This is in contrast to some of my Nobel Prize-winning lecturers who let us know in no uncertain terms that we were annoying cockroaches keeping them from their important work in the laboratory.

I believe it was his small gestures that caused students to admire him almost to the point of worship. I was the recipient of such a gesture and have never forgotten it. Eakin liked to visit his labs and chat with his students as they were working. I was slaving over a hot microscope one afternoon, trying to figure out a way to impress my lab partner, Sandy, who was a premed and much smarter than I was. We were talking animatedly about some fine point of the 48-hour chick embryo when I suddenly became aware of a presence behind me. Eakin was a big man with an academic slouch who loomed over you. I turned around, saw him, and immediately became flustered. My first thought was "I'm doomed! He's going to ask me something about when the mesoderm appears, I'll look like an idiot, and Sandy will *never* go out with me." Instead, he smiled, asked my name, then inquired, "What have you seen today that's beautiful?" I was thunderstruck. I had been aware that the things we were looking at had a wonderful, painterly quality, but I didn't know those were permissible thoughts—I thought our only job was to memorize vocabulary and state principles. Well, I was an amateur photographer, and his question opened the floodgates. I spouted about composition, and color, and how I would photograph these objects. I blathered on, and when I ran out of breath, Eakin thanked me and left the room. As he did, and Sandy looked at me with an interest I hadn't seen before, I had the unsettling feeling that I had just been visited by God, or at least, someone who was very much like Him.

Eakin's Last Lecture was legendary, and students who had taken his course in previous years would come back to hear it again and be inspired. The lecture was a reminiscence of a life in science and the joy and thrill of having the opportunity, as a young man, to work in laboratories where discoveries about the fundamental nature of life were being made. He made a point of the fact that he had not been some sort of geeky supergenius as a youngster, but had instead been blessed with a strong sense of curiosity. I can still recall being amazed by that—surely such a man must have been an exceptional student? Why, that might mean that *I* might do such things some day.

Eakin always began his lectures by acknowledging the class and saying "Good morning." This day, he did not. As he drew to the end of The Last Lecture, I remember almost being on fire. Not only did I want to do the things he did, I wanted to *be like him*—a scientist, but also a humane teacher.

For this lecture, the house lights were off, and the only illumination was provided by the lights onstage. He gave us what amounted to a benediction, a wish that we go out and build on what we had learned and have a kind of life that he had been privileged to have. Then he paused, looked out over the class with an expression of ineffable kindness, and said, "Good morning—and goodbye." The stage lights crashed off, and when the house lights came up, he was gone.

A tough act to follow.

When I started teaching large classes, I decided to do my own Last Lecture, even though it is not the custom at my college. I can heartily recommend the exercise to you, but I can't give you any suggestions for themes or subjects because, by its very nature, it is personal. I've tried various themes over the years, and I think the most successful one has been The Last Lecture for my major's course. At that point in the semester, just before finals, many of my students are running scared, they've met the first real academic challenge they've ever had, and they badly need a confidence builder. I have the "advantage" of having been a particularly rotten student as a college freshman, so I just tell them about my freshman year 40-plus years ago. I was scared just like they were, and it seemed that the harder I tried, the worse off I was. As I look out over the class, I can see the looks of recognition—and amazement. I finish off very simply: "If a kid who had a 1.8 average at the end of his first semester could end up here, so can you. Good morning—and goodbye." Lights out, and I'm gone. I've had many students come to me afterward and say they would have dropped out of college but for that lecture, so it must strike a resonant chord with at least some of them.

So this has been my Last Lecture for you. Teaching large classes well is the most difficult and challenging task in academia and offers the fewest tangible rewards. Knowing, however, that you have a real, positive, and inspiring effect on hundreds or thousands of young people will more than compensate for the liabilities. Do it right, and you will have former students all over the world who will be grateful to you for the wisdom you gave them.

READINGS AND RESOURCES

Books

There are many books on teaching in general, but few specifically on college teaching and its skills. The following books I have found to be stimulating, useful, outrage-producing, or some combination.

Brookfield, S. D. (1995). *Becoming a critically reflective teacher.* San Francisco, CA: Jossey-Bass.

> Brookfield's basic message is know thyself, and he argues that the path to excellent teaching is to be found more through thinking about how you want to teach, rather than in mastery of teaching techniques.

Charlton, J. (Ed.). (1994). *A little learning is a dangerous thing.* New York, NY: St. Martin's Press.

> A collection of delightful epigrams about teaching and learning. One of my favorites is, "A professor is one who talks in someone else's sleep" (W. H. Auden).

Corson, R., & Glavin, J. (2001). *Stage makeup* (9th ed.). Needham Heights, MA: Allyn & Bacon.

> Undoubtedly overkill for most large-class instructors, this is nevertheless *the* book on makeup for teacher-as-actor. From time to time, I give lectures in character (Pasteur, Darwin, Freud) just for the heck of it, and this book has proved to be invaluable.

Davis, B. G. (1993). *Tools for teaching.* San Francisco, CA: Jossey-Bass.

> This general book by the dean of educational development at Berkeley is a counterpart of McKeachie and Svinicki (2006) below, and covers a wide range of teaching issues.

Erickson, B. L., Peters, C. B., & Strommer, D. W. (2006). *Teaching first-year college students* (Rev. & expanded ed.). San Francisco, CA: Jossey-Bass.

Conflict-of-interest warning! Bette Erickson was my mentor in this whole large-class business (even though she's younger than I am) when I first started getting interested in learning theory and related topics. Bette and Diane did a lot of research on our freshmen at Rhode Island and used that information as the basis for the book. Recently updated for a new generation of students, some eternal truths are presented here, particularly the observation that in the life of the freshman student, your class is probably the least important thing.

Haladyna, T. M. (1996). *Writing test items to evaluate higher order thinking*. Needham Heights, MA: Allyn & Bacon.

Some of the techniques are only suitable for small classes, but if you want to go beyond testing simple memorization, there are some good suggestions here.

Hooper, J. K. (1997). *Effective slide presentations: A practical guide to more powerful presentations*. Golden, CO: Fulcrum.

If you are going to be producing many of your own visual aids, whether for PowerPoint, conventional 35mm slides, or overheads, you'll need something that will contain a discussion of graphic standards and visibility. Most of the PowerPoint books I've seen are a bit light on this topic, and you are more likely to find this kind of information in an older slide presentation book such as this.

Lowman, J. (2000). *Mastering the techniques of teaching* (2nd ed.). San Francisco, CA: Jossey-Bass.

This book is addressed more to the small-class environment but is nevertheless a good general reference.

McKeachie, W. J., & Svinicki, M. (2006). *Teaching tips: Strategies, research, and theory for college and university teachers* (12th ed.). New York, NY: Houghton Mifflin.

If there is such a thing as a "standard" book on college teaching, this is it. Particularly appropriate for small classes, there is a brief chapter on large classes. Recent editions seem to be longer on theory and shorter on tips than earlier ones.

Perry, W. G., Jr. (1999). *Forms of intellectual and ethical development in the college years: A scheme*. San Francisco, CA: Jossey-Bass.

This densely written and orotund book taught me more about why my students act the way they do than any other single work. Especially when you have freshman classes, it is very frustrating to find that when you try to encourage students to think for themselves, many of them actively resist you, and as a matter of fact become very huffy about it—"it is *your job* to tell me what I should learn, and you are a lousy teacher if you don't do it." Perry outlines a series of what he calls "positions" that students pass through as they (and if they) intellectually mature. A bit dated now (the studies were done in the 1950s and 1960s on a limited group of students—males at Harvard), the general ideas still ring true to me. I found this book a great source of comfort. Freshmen *really are* different from juniors and seniors and cannot be expected to respond the same way to a given teaching technique.

Persig, R. M. (1974). *Zen and the art of motorcycle maintenance: An inquiry into values.* New York, NY: William Morrow.

Impossible to categorize narrowly, this is a travelogue, treatise on philosophy, and exploration of families and mental health. I included it because the author/narrator takes a college teaching job in Montana and has some thought-provoking observations about teaching and teaching techniques.

Popham, W. J. (1999). *Modern educational measurement: Practical guidelines for educational leaders* (3rd ed.). Needham Heights, MA: Allyn & Bacon.

Intended for schools rather than colleges, it is nonetheless useful if you wish to explore reliability and validity in depth.

Sacks, P. (1996). *Generation X goes to college: An eye-opening account of teaching in postmodern America.* Chicago, IL: Open Court.

The pseudonymous Sacks, a journalist by trade, decides to try teaching in a community college for a while. After having been there for a semester or two, he realizes he has a potential book on his hands and starts taking detailed notes about his interactions with the (his sentiments) apathetic, entitled, boorish, anti-intellectual "students" in his class. I desperately wanted to disagree with him, but for every anecdote he recounted, I could match and raise him one. In 2007, with the Millennial Generation, the situation is, if anything, more extreme than his portrayal. However, I believe the picture is more balanced than he presents. The problem in big, lower division courses is not just the presence of slack-jawed place-sitters, but how to address their requirements and needs as well as those of the ambitious wisdom-seekers sitting next to them.

Stanley, C. A., & Porter M. E. (Eds.). (2002). *Engaging large classes: Strategies and techniques for college faculty.* Bolton, MA: Anker.

A collection of 29 essays by different large-class authors discussing both theoretical issues involving teaching and practical matters. More of a reference than a guidebook.

Stout, M. (2000). *The feel-good curriculum: The dumbing down of America's kids in the name of self-esteem.* Cambridge, MA: Da Capo Press.

> This is one of those books that makes you say, "Aha! So that's why they're the way they are." Your colleagues in the College of Education are guaranteed not to like this book. However, it makes a plausible case to explain the low expectation of work and high expectation of reward that is so often seen in first-year college students coming out of the public school system.

Timpson, W. M., Burgoyne, S., Jones, C. S., & Jones, W. (1997). *Teaching and performing: Ideas for energizing your classes.* Madison, WI: Magna.

> If you can get past the absolute dead seriousness, and attempt to give scholarly dignity to what is often intentionally making a fool of yourself in front of 300 people, the book has many good suggestions. As compensation, a series of self-help book exercises in acting technique are spliced in. Be prepared to do some heavy skimming, however.

Tufte, E. R. (2001). *Visual display of quantitative information* (2nd ed.). Cheshire, CT: Graphics Press.

> Required reading for anyone who has to present numerical information graphically. A beautiful book.

Tufte, E. R. (2006). *The cognitive style of PowerPoint: Pitching out corrupts within* (2nd ed.). Cheshire, CT: Graphics Press.

> A contrarian's view of PowerPoint: He hates it and has some pretty good reasons for feeling that way.

Movies

The following is a personal selection of my favorite movies about teaching. Inclusion on the list does not imply cinematic greatness—some of these turkeys are really dogs. They all have something to say about teaching, however, even if just a commentary about how dreadful some teachers can be.

Cheaters. (2000). Jeff Daniels. John Stockwell (Director). United States: Home Box Office.

> Morally challenged high school teacher helps his kids cheat their way to an academic championship. Based on a true story, this is a very disturbing film for faculty concerned with academic cheating. Viewed from a cheating student's

perspective, it shows the rationalizations students use to justify their actions. No shame, no remorse, and the only regret is getting caught.

Dead Poet's Society. (1989). Robin Williams. Peter Weir (Director). United States: Buena Vista.

Manic Old Boy returns to teach at his old prep school and finds redemption and disgrace. The Williams character finds a variety of ingenious ways to interest his studly preppies in something they would normally hold in high disdain—poetry. Too late, however, he finds that churlish administrators have more clout than charismatic renegades, and he has to accept his walking papers to the accompaniment of loud huzzahs from his former charges.

Educating Rita. (1983). Michael Caine, Julie Walters. Lewis Gilbert (Director). United States: Columbia Pictures.

Burned-out alcoholic English professor of literature tutors a returning-to-school hairdresser. One of the best depictions of the magic that can happen when a professor truly connects with a student and a mind is enlightened. A ripping good story, with a non-Hollywood ending, too.

Finding Forrester. (2000). Sean Connery. Gus van Sant (Director). United States: Columbia Pictures.

Reclusive writer takes brilliant ghetto kid under his wing and teaches him how to write. A little slow and follows the model of *Educating Rita*, but first-time actor Robert Brown does an amazing acting turn as the kid.

Goodbye, Mr. Chips. (1939). Robert Donat, Greer Garson. Sam Wood (Director). United States: MGM.

The original beloved-teacher film. It is laughably corny by today's standards, but I still cry every time I see it because I had teachers like Mr. Chips, and I suspect that many of us who take teaching seriously would like to be a bit like him.

The Paper Chase. (1973). John Houseman, Lindsay Wagner, Timothy Bottoms. James Bridges (Director). United States: 20th Century Fox.

Brilliant and intimidating college teacher makes his students feel like worms. No, lower than worms. Set at Harvard Law School. Good classroom scenes, if you are into humiliation. I had a teacher just like the monstrous Houseman character when I was a freshman.

Real Genius. (1985). Val Kilmer, William Atherton, Gabriel Jarret. Martha Coolidge (Director). United States: Tristar Pictures.

> Brilliant but naive college science students hornswoggled by manipulative professor. My first reaction to this film, set in an institution suspiciously resembling Cal Tech, was that it was a documentary. The pranks, the pressures, the insane workloads all rang true from my freshman year at RPI (before I escaped to Berkeley). Made during the 1980s, when 1960s and 1970s era college students were now making Hollywood movies (*Pretty in Pink, The Breakfast Club, Fast Times at Ridgemont High, War Games, Ferris Bueller's Day Off*). Every adult in this film is a boor, a fool, or works for the CIA. There are a few choice bits of business involving lectures that make it a worthwhile view.

Stand and Deliver. (1988). Edward James Olmos. Ramón Menéndez (Director). United States: Warner Brothers.

> Tough teacher takes no prisoners, wins success for all. Loosely based on a true story. A successful Latino engineer, Jaime Escalante, takes a try at teaching math in a barrio high school in Los Angeles. Convinced that his kids can rise to meet a challenge if they are offered one, he forms an Advanced Placement calculus class. All of his kids pass the national exam and (surprise!) the AP board challenges the results, feeling that the barrio kids must have cheated. They retake the test and all pass again. Escalante exits triumphantly. The Escalante character is tough and no-nonsense but has a heart of gold. Five stars in the feel-good category. The only thing they don't tell you in the movie is that the real students were hand-picked, and there were a lot of dropouts, but it's still a great message—and a good and very funny movie.

Wonder Boys. (2000). Michael Douglas, Frances McDormand, Tobey Maguire, Robert Downey, Jr. Curtis Hanson (Director). United States: Paramount Pictures.

> Burned-out author/English teacher revitalized by eccentric but brilliant student. One of the first things one of my senior colleagues told me after I made tenure was that I could now essentially do anything I wanted to do and never be fired, with one exception: I should never have an affair with a dean's wife. Times have changed but the advice still holds, as Michael Douglas's character finds, except now *he* has the affair with a female dean. Almost a screwball comedy, the tone of faculty life and politics is surprisingly well captured.

There are almost as many movies about teachers as about vampires (well, that's not exactly true—I've found only about 100 movies about teachers, but the Master Vampyre List has almost 2,000 vampire movie postings). Whatever the number, I can recommend these additional films as having something instructive to say about teaching and learning.

- *Animal House* (1978)

- *Blackboard Jungle* (1955)

- *Children of a Lesser God* (1986)

- *Dangerous Minds* (1995)

- *The Faculty* (1998)

- *Mr. Holland's Opus* (1995)

- *October Sky* (1999)

- *Renaissance Man* (1994)

- *Teachers* (1984)

- *To Sir, with Love* (1967)

Web Sites

Web sites are like floating crap games in New York: No matter how big and flashy they are, they'll probably be gone tomorrow. As URLs frequently change, I have included keyword titles instead of addresses. A search engine like Google or AltaVista should lead you to the address. These sites were up at the time I listed them—no guarantees beyond that. In recent years there has been a proliferation of sites dealing with large-class teaching, so much so that you can now waste a significant amount of your time browsing sites and going down endless link pathways. There is also a wide variety of newsgroups and chat groups available—I cut way back on my participation when I started having to sort through 60 or 70 postings a day looking for the elusive nugget of valuable information. Some people love them, though.

- "Center Advancement Teaching Illinois Tips"
  A good listing of books and other resources from the University of Illinois.

- "Large Class FAQ"
  A frequently-asked-questions site from the University of Pennsylvania's Center for Excellence in Learning and Teaching.

- "Large Class Project"
  A good, indexed links site from the University of Central Florida.

- "Large Class Resource Links"

A good links page from the University of Oregon's Teaching Improvement Center.

- "Large Class Resources"
  A very good links and articles site from the University of Maryland's Center for Teaching Excellence.

- "Making Large Lecture Classes Interactive"
  A bibliography of older (pre-1990s) print articles from Northwestern University.

- "Students Who Don't Study"
  I hope this is still up by the time you read this. Henry Bauer is a wonderfully curmudgeonly retired chemistry professor who wrote this treatise in 1996.

- "Teaching Large Classes"
  A small links site that contains some links not cited in the previous sites. From the University of Buffalo.

- "Teaching Large Classes"
  A collection of short articles with ideas on making large classes more interactive. From Wright State University.

- "Teaching with Electronic Technology"
  An excellent, comprehensive links site from the University of Maryland.

- "Web Grade Sheet"
  A web-based grading system. No guarantees on this one—I haven't tried it myself, but if you're a webbie, it looks interesting.

Newsletters
Neither of these subscription newsletters specializes in large classes, and both are a bit pricey, but I have found the occasional good suggestion in both.

- *The National Teaching and Learning Forum*
  www.ntlf.com

- *The Teaching Professor*
  www.teachingprofessor.com

Publishers Specializing in Teaching and Learning

- Heldref Publications (www.heldref.org)
  Sponsors a variety of journals on higher education topics, such as *College Teaching* and *The Journal of Educational Research*.

- Jossey-Bass (www.josseybass.com)
  Large list of publications relating to higher education. Good source for books about teaching and learning in colleges.

Journals Dealing with or Frequently Having Articles on College Teaching

- *American Biology Teacher*

- *Art Education*

- *Change*

- *Communication Education*

- *History Teacher*

- *Journal of Basic Writing*

- *Journal of Chemical Education*

- *Journal of College Science Teaching*

- *Journal of Economic Education*

- *Journal of Education for Business*

- *Journal of Geological Education*

- *Journal of Higher Education*

- *Journal of Management Education*

- *Journal of Research in College Teaching*

- *Journal on Excellence in College Teaching*

- *New Directions for Higher Education*

- *Physics Education*

- *Review of Higher Education*

- *Review of Research in Higher Education*

- *Science Education*

- *Teaching of Psychology*

- *Teaching Philosophy*

- *Teaching Political Science*

- *Teaching Sociology*

National Agencies Funding College Teaching Innovations

- Andrew W. Mellon Foundation

- Carnegie Foundation for the Advancement of Teaching

- Fund for the Improvement of Postsecondary Education

- Howard Hughes Medical Institute

- Lilly Foundation

- National Science Foundation

Appendix A

Sample Course Outline

This is the entire information manual given to students on the first day of a nonscience major's general biology course. Every course is different, but this will give you an idea of what can be included.

Biology 104B
Information Manual

Welcome to Biology 104B. We hope you will find this course interesting and useful. This manual will give you the information you need to understand course rules and procedures and contains suggestions you may find helpful in getting the most out of the course.

Instructor's information:
Name: Dr. Frank Heppner
Office: A119 Biological Sciences Center
Phone: 555-8741
Office hours: Announced at first lecture and posted on instructor's office window.
Place to leave messages: Biological Sciences Department Office, BISC

Lab teaching assistants' information:
Name: Announced at first lab.
Office and office hours: Announced at first lab.
Place for labs: A-118, BISC

Text: Announced at first lecture, obtainable at campus bookstore and RI Books.

Equipment needed: None.

Amount of study: *A student with an average college reading ability will need to spend approximately 6 hours a week outside of class in reading, working problems, and preparation for laboratories.* Reading the texts should take only a relatively small amount of time. Most of your time will be spent in outlining, answering end-of-chapter questions, problem sets, etc. If you find yourself spending significantly less time in preparation than 6 hours a week, it is highly probably that you are studying incorrectly.

Late work: Assignments to be turned in are expected on time. *Late work will not be accepted and will be graded as a zero.* Students prepared to offer *documented proof* that circumstances entirely beyond their control resulted in lateness may apply for an exemption to this rule. Documented proof may include but is not limited to the following items (all on official stationery): doctor's report, counseling center report, health center report, police report, death notice (for attendance at funerals), wake announcement (for attendance at wakes), coach's letter (for team absences), etc. *Students should* always *make copies of computer discs or papers that are to be turned in.* "I lost my paper" or "I erased my disc" are examples of nonacceptable reasons for missing deadlines.

Study skills workshop: Some of you may be unfamiliar with the skills needed for success in university science courses. During the first full week of classes, there will be an evening, one-hour workshop on the skills required for Biology 104B. The time and place of this workshop will be announced at the first lecture. Attendance is not required at this workshop, but is strongly recommended.

Lecture attendance: Students who do not regularly attend all lectures will find themselves at a severe disadvantage, and their grades will probably be adversely affected.

Responsibility for announcements: From time to time, announcements about course changes are made during lecture or laboratory. Students arriving late, or missing lectures or laboratories, are responsible for obtaining such announcements. Students are responsible for the consequences of missing announcements.

Missed labs: If you miss a lab, first contact your teaching assistant to discuss any missed work, then try to attend any of the other labs offered during the week—a list is posted outside the lab door.

Term papers: Term papers and lab reports must be on topics exactly as assigned by TAs. Papers not on assigned topics will not be accepted. The format of papers must be exactly as outlined in lab, or they will not be accepted. Any paper not adequately defended at the assigned time for the oral defense will be graded zero.

Cheating: Cheating, either copying on exams or plagiarism on papers, will not be tolerated. Punishments for cheating range up to expulsion from the university with a permanent notation on the student's record of that fact. Students should familiarize themselves with the definition of plagiarism from the university manual. Examples of plagiarism include failing to acknowledge the source of ideas in the body of the text of a term paper as well as failing to quote passages taken directly from a source.

**Cheating is property theft and will be treated accordingly.
Don't do the crime if you can't do the time!**

Makeup: If you know in advance that you will be unable to take a lecture exam or quiz, for example if you have an unavoidable physician's appointment, contact the course instructor or TA as soon as you know that you will be unable to attend. Makeup work can usually be arranged. If an emergency situation arises immediately before an exam or quiz, notify the appropriate instructor as soon as the emergency is resolved. If alternate arrangements are not made, missed assignments will count zero.

Help sessions: At various times during the week, voluntary help sessions will be offered. The purpose of the help sessions is to allow you to ask questions in a small, informal context and to have the opportunity to have your knowledge checked. Past experience has suggested that students who regularly attend at least one recitation section a week, and participate in the discussions, perform at a grade higher level than those who do not attend. These sessions are *not* tutoring and will be of little help to students who do not attend lectures or who have not kept up on the reading.

Testing: You will have a short mini-exam, two one-hour examinations, and one final examination, which will cover text readings and the material given in lectures. The standard format for these examinations is multiple choice. If you prefer a different format for your examination, for example an essay exam or an oral exam, let the course instructor know at least a week before the exam so an alternate can be prepared. The hour exams will each have 30 questions, and the final exam will have 80 questions. Some the these questions will involve problem solving as well as memorization and may have multiple parts. In the laboratory, you will have a mixture of quizzes, laboratory practical exams, and term papers. Each lab will be slightly different, depending on the practices of the teaching assistant in charge. Points will be awarded the various assignments according to the following schedule:

	Points
Mini exam	20
1st hour exam	60
2nd hour exam	60
Final exam	160
Laboratory	150
Total	*450*

Retesting: On either of the hour examinations, if you were not satisfied with your score, you may wait a minimum of a week (but no later than three weeks) and retake an examination covering the same material as the original examination. However, the second examination will be essay format, rather than multiple choice. Your score on the retake examination will *replace* your original score—the two will *not* be averaged. You will thus want to be reasonably sure that your second score will be higher than the first.

Grading: The grading system in Biology 104B is noncompetitive and is based 100% on performance. Every member of the class can get an A (or every member of the class can get an F) under this system. The following are the targets you should aim for if you wish a certain letter grade:

	%
A	85
A–	81
B+	75
B	72
B–	69
C+	67
C	64
C–	61
D+	58
D	55

1. To earn a D (pass) in Biology 104B, the student must demonstrate a satisfactory knowledge of the vocabulary of the subject and show that he or she has, at a minimum, performed all the reading and lab assignments. His or her attendance record in the laboratories shall be satisfactory to the instructor and all assignments will be turned in.

2. To earn a C in Biology 104B, in addition to the above, the student will demonstrate that he or she can solve simple problems in animal biology and has a basic grasp of the general principles covered in the lecture and reading assignments, such as genetics, ecology, behavior, etc. All assignments shall be performed on time.

3. To earn a B in Biology 104B, in addition to the above, the student will consistently solve more difficult problems and show, by questions asked and participation in class discussion, that he or she is fully familiar with the principles covered in assignments. His or her writing ability, as shown in term papers, will be good and without major flaws in English.

4. To receive an A in Biology 104B, in addition to the above, the student will be able to solve difficult and complex problems, integrating materials from the course and his or her own background in order to arrive at comprehensive answers. His or her written assignments will be imaginative and well thought out and he or she will demonstrate a high degree of creativity and participation in the laboratory.

You will notice two things about this distribution. First, it doesn't follow the "traditional" 90–100 = A pattern. This is not due to the instructor's generosity, but is a reflection of the fact that the material in Biology 104B is more demanding than in many courses and exam averages tend to be slightly lower. You will also note that the biggest "jump" between grades is between B+ and A–. This is because, like a gold medal in the Olympics, an A in Biology 104B is a mark of a rare distinction and achievement. It is, frankly, difficult to attain, and for this reason a student who earns an A in Biology 104B is entitled to a good deal of pride and respect from his or her fellows. Second, it should also be observed that with this grading system, if the whole class does well, the whole class will get good grades. There are no "quotas" on the better grades as there is in a system that "curves" or "scales" grades. In a "curve" grading system, if someone else's score goes up, your grade goes down—he or she has raised the average. In the Biology 104B system, it is to your advantage to help other students because helping someone else helps you. Think of it as being part of the same team.

There are only two circumstances in which we will award a higher grade to a student than would be indicated by his or her final percentage score. If a student is very close to the border of the next higher grade, and started poorly at the beginning of the semester but was performing consistently at a much higher level by the end of the semester, we reserve the right to boost that student's grade, thereby rewarding improvement. Similarly, if a student is performing at a consistently high level, but has, for example, one disastrous quiz that pulls him or her below the border of a grade *and* we are aware that some external factor, for example a family emergency or illness, in all probability pulled the student down on that occasion, we *may* take that factor into consideration. This exception will rarely be granted and will *not* be considered in the case of a poor performance on a major exam, for which other procedures (makeups, etc.) are available for emergencies.

The assignments have been set up so that the best grades do not necessarily go to the students with the best memories. Problem-solving skills are equally important.

Extra credit: No "extra credit" is available in Biology 104B.

Students who are bored because they've had it already: Biology 104B is a big course, and the students in it come from various backgrounds. If you have had a good AP biology course and can demonstrate that you have retained a level of knowledge equivalent to what Biology 104B offers, contact the course instructor at the earliest possible opportunity. We are very flexible and can custom tailor reading assignments, examinations, etc. You have to make yourself known to us first, though. Science majors should really take Biology 113; 104B is not designed for your needs.

Students with science fear: A very common problem. There are techniques to deal with this. Identify yourself, privately if you wish, to your TA or the course instructor, and we can help.

Students who find themselves overwhelmed by study demands: Again, a very common problem. As with science fear, we can help, but only if you identify yourself to us.

Foreign students with English problems: Identify yourself to your TA and course instructor. There are certain things we can do to assist you.

Suggestions, criticisms, comments: Biology 104B is constantly changing and experimenting with approaches and procedures. Some of these changes may not work, and we want to know if something's wrong.

End-of-semester travel: Do not make end-of-semester travel plans until you have determined when the final examination will be.

Students with disabilities requesting accommodations: Students requesting accommodations should see the instructor sometime during the first week of class. Accommodation requests must be presented in a timely fashion in writing with approval from the Disabilities Services Office—an accommodation request made at the last minute may not be possible to arrange. The Office of Disability Services for Students (555-2098) will be happy to assist you.

Expectations for Biology 104B: When we say we "expect" you to know something, this is what we mean:

Vocabulary
You are responsible for the definitions of all boldfaced words in the text. "Responsible" means that you should be able to provide a brief definition upon

request or be able to recognize the correct definition from a list of incorrect definitions. You are also responsible for technical terms defined in lecture.

Concepts

You are responsible for the major concepts outlined in lecture plus the major concepts listed in the chapter summary. A concept is an idea, hypothesis, or description, like respiration, glycolysis, monohybrid cross, ecological niche, etc. A concept may either be broad, like cell division, or narrow, like mitosis. Your responsibility for concepts is:

1. Be able to provide a definition of the concept.

2. Be able to provide an example or recognize an unfamiliar example of the concept.

3. Be able to explain the significance of the concept—e.g., glycolysis is the process that provides the initial breakdown of food materials.

4. In the case of a process, like the Krebs cycle, be able to explain how the process works, including the materials fed into the process, what happens to them in the process, and what the products of the process are.

It will be assumed that you have done any problem sets and answered all questions at the ends of chapters.

The goal of Biology 104B: A thorough knowledge of modern biology is enormously important to every person living in a technological society, and it is not too much of an exaggeration to say that the fate of the United States is linked to the scientific literacy of its people. We take great pride in offering Biology 104B to you, and we hope you take equal pride in your participation.

Prof. Frank Heppner
For the Staff of Biology 104B

Appendix B

First-Day Checklist

Checklist Zoology 111

Day Before Class

___ Check out auditorium: projectors, mike, etc.
___ Remind TAs to be there.
___ Remind AV about camera folks.
___ Get rosters from office.
___ Check cameras, white balance.
___ Align switcher.
___ Check battery supply.
___ Check projector bulb supply.
___ Lecture notes okay? Last minute notes?
___ Walk-through for timing and camera marks.
___ Check music tape.
___ Check title slide.
___ Check transparency supply.
___ Check handout supply:
   ___ syllabus
   ___ course outline
   ___ problem set
   ___ affidavit

Just Before Lecture

___ Check the goods:
   ___ mike
   ___ spare battery
   ___ spare bulbs
   ___ handouts
   ___ transparency sheets
   ___ overhead pens
   ___ regular pen
   ___ videotape
   ___ roster
   ___ lecture notes

___ scratch paper
___ title slides
___ Set up cameras:
   ___ WB
   ___ load tape
   ___ marks and frames
___ Set up audiotape:
   ___ cue
   ___ set for overload
___ Check mike level.
___ Set house lights.
___ Set stage lights.
___ Set title slide.
___ Set switcher for dissolve from title to A cam, cut to B cam.
___ Crew ready?
   ___ cue checks
___ Mike on standby.

Five Minutes

___ Head. Last call. Check fly.
___ Punch up audio.
___ Dim house light.
___ Entrance: house lights down 1, stage lights up 6.
___ It's *show time!*

APPENDIX C

SAMPLE COURSE SYLLABUS

Biology 104B
Spring 2000

Date	Lecture	Lab	Reading (alters)
January			
18	Introduction	No Lab	1, 2
20	What Is Science?		
25	What Is Life?	Introduction	3, 4
27	Death and Forensic Biology		
February			
1	Death and Forensic Biology	Doing Science	6, 8
3	*Mini-exam* and Human Chemistry		9, 10
10	Human Chemistry		
15	How Your Body Works	Microscopy	27, 28, 29
17	How Your Body Works		
24	*1st Exam*	Osmosis	30, 31, 32
29	How Your Body Works	Mitosis, Karyotype	

Date	Lecture	Lab	Reading (alters)
March			
2	Family Biology		33, 34, 35
7	Family Biology	Genetics	
9	Family Biology		36, 11
15	Break		
17	Break		
21	Health and Disease	Predator-Prey	12, 13
	Health and Disease		
28	Pseudoscience	Social Issues	18, 19
30	Food Biology		
April			
4	Food Biology	Animal Diversity	22, 38
6	*2nd Exam*		
11	Food Biology	Natural Selection	14, 39
13	Fierce Creatures		
18	Fierce Creatures	To Be Announced	15, 40
20	Saving the Whales		
25	Saving the Whales	Environmental Field	16, 41
27	Origins Biology		
May			
2	Is It the Truth? Or Is It Bull----?		

Examination responsibilities: For the *mini-exam*, you are responsible for Chapters 1, 2, 3, 4, and all lectures through February 1. For the 1st exam, you are responsible for all of the above, plus Chapters 6, 8, 9, 10, 26, 27, 28, 29, plus all lectures through February 17. For the second examination, you are responsible for all of the above, plus Chapters 11, 12, 13, 18, 19, 30, 31, 32, 33, 34, 35, 36, plus all lectures through April 4. For the final examination, you are responsible for all assigned chapters and all lectures.

Appendix D

Sample First-Day Lecture

Zoology 111

Stage Directions
[Comments]

[As will shortly be obvious, this first lecture reflects a distinctive personal style of lecture presentation. It suits me and my class; it may not be appropriate for you and yours. However, there are certain elements of information that should be presented in *any* first lecture, and it may be instructive to see how they are integrated with this particular style. The stage directions here reflect the use of television cameras, but in a class without cameras "Cut to camera B" would mean the instructor shifts position and directs attention to a different part of the class].

A large, 400-seat auditorium. The stage is bare except for a cart on which are several TV monitors and an electronic overhead projector. A teaching assistant is in the projection booth to operate the stage lights, and the two TV cameras in front of the stage area are operated by technicians from information technology. The lecture is to begin at 9:00a.m. A title/logo slide is projected on the large screen via a video projector. It says "Zoology 111" and depicts geese taking flight. At 8:57 students are still coming in, some unsure of the class location. At exactly 8:58, the house lights dim slightly and over the loudspeaker booms the first strains of the theme from Star Wars. *Normally, the music is timed to end at exactly the stroke of the hour, but on the first day, it ends at 9:03:58 to allow stragglers to come in. On the last beat of the music, the house lights dim further (but remain bright enough to write), and the stage lights are raised.* LECTURER *makes his entrance stage right. He is dressed in a pin-striped English-cut suit, with a pastel blue shirt and club tie. He walks up to the cart and stands next to it, not behind it. The A camera operator controls the video switcher, and when* LECTURER *is in place, dissolves away from the title slide to a head-and-shoulders shot of* LECTURER.

Cheery and bright. Good morning, ladies and gentlemen, I am Professor Frank Heppner, and I will be your instructor for Zoology 111. *Superimpose title slide "Heppner."* [New college students are often anxious about how they should address this new kind of person called a professor. It helps if you guide them a bit, but it doesn't really matter what you call yourself—Mr., Ms., Professor, Doctor, Jane, or whatever.] On behalf of the Department of Biological Sciences, and our entire teaching staff, I want to welcome you to the course that will be the most interesting, *pause*, **challenging**, and ultimately rewarding one you will take all semester. Zoology 111 marks the beginning of a long and winding road that leads to some of the most respected and responsible professions in the world.

Now, I know you have many questions, especially those of you who are new to the university, and I hope that before the hour is up, I will have answered most if not all of them. If there's anything you're unsure about, it's kind of scary to raise your hand in front of all these people, so we'll finish a couple of minutes early so you can come up and ask me in private and still get to your next class.

Slight position shift. Cut to camera B. Zoology 111 is a pre-professional and world-class course. Let me explain what I mean by that. It is a pre-professional course because it is intended for people who aspire to professional careers related to the biological sciences. There are many of these, and we literally have majors A to Z represented here—animal science to zoology. At any one time, we will have maybe 20 different majors here. ONE MINUTE ELAPSED TIME. In the fall semester, we usually have more pharmacy majors than any other. Raise hands, how many pharmacists here? Whoa! They're gonna have to increase aspirin production to keep all you guys busy. *Points to student in middle of audience.* You're a pharmacy major, right? Where are you from? Pawtucket! A pharmacist from Pawtucket. So you're going to peddle pills in Pawtucket. Terrific. Welcome to Zoo 111. [This little bit of business is very important. In the first minute of the class, they find out that although this is a big lecture, it's going to be interactive and it is painless to respond to a question from LECTURER.] Well, there are two things that all of you have in common, whether you want to be doctors or save whales. The first is that you're all going to have to take other biology courses in the future. And all these courses have something in common. [This is a standard technique in public speaking, especially political speeches and sermons. Take the same phrase, like "in common," and repeat it two or three times.] They have in common that they're harder than Zoology 111, and they assume that you learned certain things when you took Zoo 111; things like definitions, vocabulary terms, parts of the body, kinds of hormones, and so forth. They just *assume* you learned these things here, and build on it. That's why Zoology 111 is so important, and why you need to try your very best here—it will make a huge difference to your future. [There will be a small but totally clueless group of students who have no idea why they're in your class. Not all of these students are stupid—some are just naïve, and need things spelled out for them.] *Walks over to other side of cart.*

The second thing almost all of you have in common is a need for your introductory biology course to be as thorough and comprehensive as it can be, because most of you, in three or four years, will be taking a standardized test of your knowledge of biology. TWO MINUTES ELAPSED TIME. For premeds it's the M-Cat exam. For pharmacists, it's the pharmacy boards. And for these exams, it is what you have *learned* in Zoo 111, not what your grade was, that is important. [*Every* group of students needs a pitch in the first couple of minutes about why it is personally important to them to invest time and effort in your course. For majors, it is easy—you can talk about careers. For nonmajors in general education, you have to be more creative. When I teach nonscience majors in a general biology course, I ask them the rhetorical question, "Why should an ordinary person have at least some knowledge of the science of biology?" They are then immediately broken into six-person "juries" and given an aggravated rape case in which the key evidence involves DNA identification. I allow each of the juries to vote, based on the evidence presented. Naturally, the decisions are all over the place—some guilty, some not guilty, some hung. I then ask them, "Suppose you knew a little more about DNA? Do you think you would understand the evidence better and be able to give a better, more consistent decision?" They generally answer in the affirmative, then I say, "Well *that's* why you are taking Biology 102, because this was a real case and real people just like yourselves had to decide it."]

Walks over to other side of cart. Cut to camera A. [You can use your body as a kind of visual punctuation mark to reinforce what you say.] Now, what do I mean by "world-class course"? Well, it is an unfortunate fact of life that many of the fields you aspire to are highly competitive. Raise hands, how many premeds here today? Okay, when you guys [choice of pronoun is important here: "you people" is too formal and distancing; "guys" used to apply to males, but through usage is now nongendered] apply to medical school, only about one in three of you will make it. How about pre-vets? It's even worse for you. About one in four. This proves that vets have to be smarter than doctors because their patients can't talk. For you pharmacists, I can't tell you the exact odds, but like many other areas, the big drug companies are hiring a lot of low-wage people like pharmacists' assistants and not so many pharmacists. If you want to go to one of the good research grad schools, maybe one in five, and if you want one of the glamour areas, like wildlife biology or marine mammals or marine biology, fageddaboutit—maybe one in thirty or so. The problem is that these professions are very desirable, so a lot of people want to go into them, but there aren't really that many opportunities available.

But I've got news for you. *Pause.* Your competition is not in this room. No, your neighbors here are your teammates—your allies. As a matter of fact, you should introduce yourself to the two people on either side of you, right now, because you're going to have to find study partners. Go ahead. Do it. Don't be shy. *Pauses while students introduce themselves.* [It is good to get them in the habit of thinking of a lecture as something that is active, rather than passive.] Okay, that's enough; you're just trying to get acquainted, not hook up. Yes, these folks are going to *help* you toward your goal. Your competition, the people who are going to try to *keep* you from your goals, that competition is sitting in a very similar room 35 miles to the north of here, at Brown University. [I use Brown as a convenient Hated Other because it is close and familiar. Ninety-nine percent of the college professors in the United States teach at colleges that can call upon a school with a better reputation as a Hated Other. The rest of you I can't help.] When you premeds apply for medical school, right next to your application in the stack is going to be one from a Harvard graduate. When you pharmacy majors apply for a job with CVS [local major pharmacy chain], right next to your application is going to be one from a graduate of the Johns Hopkins pharmacy program. When you marine biologists apply to a good graduate school, right next to your application [principle of three repetitions, three examples, etc.] will be one from a graduate of Oxford, of Cambridge, of the Sorbonne, University of Heidelberg, University of Tokyo. No, ladies and gentlemen, *pause, searching glance out over the class,* your competition is not in this room. Your competition is the WORLD! *Expansive gesture with arms, camera rapidly zooms back as his arms fly out.* [Many of my students have told me that this single remark and gesture made more of an impression on them than anything else I said in the first lecture.]

Dissolve to camera B. Now, if you are to prevail, to triumph, to win over this kind of competition, your first-year biology course is going to have to be as thorough and demanding as theirs is because you will all be taking the same standardized exam in three or four years. And in this respect I have good news and bad news for you. This is like the guy who went to the doctor for some routine tests, and a couple of days later the doctor calls him up and says, "Mr. Jones, we got your tests back, and I have some good news and bad news for you. FIVE MINUTES ELAPSED TIME. Which do you want first?" Mr. Jones says, "Well, doc, why don't you give me the good news first." "Okay, well, the tests say you have 24 hours to live." "Twenty-four hours to live! My God, doctor, if that's the good news, what's the bad news?" "Well, I tried to text you yesterday, but you didn't call back." [Every book on teaching or public speaking will tell you to use humor. However, humor in a large class is very much like poison gas. A terrific weapon, but just as likely to blow back and kill you, as kill the enemy. Until you feel *very* comfortable with your big class, I would suggest leaving humor as an advanced technique.] Well, my good news is really good news. If you do well in your biology degree at URI, you can go anywhere and do anything afterwards. [My university, very much a "second tier" one, suffers strongly from an inferiority complex. This is damaging to the students, and I quash it at every opportunity.] I'm going to read to you a list of names of students who have taken Zoology 111 before and are now wildly successful in their chosen professions. Maybe these students even sat in the seat you are sitting in. If they could do it, you can do it. *Reads off long list of distinguished grads—professors, scientists, executives, etc.* [The list is actually so long it is boring. This is intentional. The impression is that this kind of outstanding success is *routine* for Zoology 111 students.] Okay, that's the good news. Are you ready for the bad news? The bad news is that if you want to compete successfully against an MIT student, you're going to have to *work* like an MIT student. And this is where you're going to find out something now that I bet you didn't know. There are actually *two* URIs [What follows is a key passage for students who are in demanding majors. Obviously, not all colleges have this problem, but as will shortly be evident, students enrolled in demanding majors are often bewildered by the wildly varied workloads students in different majors have, and find it "unfair."]

Cut to camera A. One URI is the famous party school you've all heard about. All those stories are true. By picking the right major and the right courses, you can go through four years of URI, hardly ever open a book, party every night, and still get pretty good grades. After that? Who knows, but hey, you've had a fantastic four years. You, however, are not enrolled in *that* URI. By your choice of major, you have enrolled in the *other* URI, the famous research institution known all over the world for its marine and oceanographic programs. This explains why you might be studying until your eyeballs bleed, to barely get a B–, while your roommate is down the line [off campus] every night and gets B+s. You might say that's not fair, but it really is a matter of choice, not fairness. The other thing you might run into really isn't fair. There will be some students in this class who can scan the book and completely understand everything they read the first time. They have natural abilities in this area, just as some people have natural abilities in music and can play beautifully without ever having a lesson. But these people have nothing to do with you. You can accomplish the same things they do, the only difference being that you have to work harder than they do. That's not fair, but that's life.

Shifts position. Well, what is Zoology 111 *about?* Why, it is about LIFE! It is about birth, death, sex, violence, ungrateful children, sacrifice, cruelty, titanic battles between warring armies, deception, stealth, the devotion of parents, sickness and health, giants, blood and guts, and where we came from and where we might be going. It is *Jurassic Park, Alien, Silence of the Lambs, E.T., Indiana Jones, Hot Zone,* and *The Fly* all rolled into one, with an important difference, however. *Going* to movies is just plain fun. Zoology 111 is more like *making* movies, which is fun but incredibly hard work, and requires an enormous amount of time, study, and research. [You are pretty safe in referring to any blockbuster movie or major TV series within the last 10 years—most students have seen them. However, good luck with references to Greek mythology (unless they made a movie out of it), Shakespeare, great writers, poems, general history—the list is depressingly long.] Zoology 111 is an introduction to the biology of animals—what kinds of animals there are, how they're put together, how they work, how they relate to each other, how they affect us, and how we affect them. You will learn some amazing things. Shocking things. And yes, there will be some things—quite a few things—that you will have to memorize.

Shifts position. Students ask me all the time, *whiny voice,* "Why do we have to memorize all this crap? You can always look it up if you need to know it." Fair question. You have to memorize it because you're going to be professionals you're going to talk to other professionals, and you need to use the vocabulary that professionals use, or you'll look like a stupid idiot. LECTURER *has a small stack of books secreted on a shelf under the electronic overhead projector.* Can you imagine being a doctor, discussing a patient with another doctor. *Changes voice.* "Thanks for coming in on this one with me, Jim. Now, my patient here has a little pain in her tummy. It seems to be a couple of inches to the right of her bellybutton. Now, when I looked at her X-ray, it looked like her, oh, I never remember the name, but I can just look it up here. *Fumbles through book.* Oh, yes, they call it the I think you say it doo-oh-deen-um, whatever, it looks a little bigger than it should be, but on the other hand, that thing up near the liver, oh, you know, it's kind of green and it has something to do with fats, just a sec—*fumbles through another book.* Yes! The gallbladder, the gallbladder seems to be just a smidge enlarged too." *Changes voice back to normal.* Ridiculous, eh? Every profession has its vocabulary, and there is no way around it—that vocabulary must be memorized until it becomes second nature. Now, you represent a lot of different professions, but the vocabulary of Zoology 111 is common to almost all of them, so that's why I have to ask you to memorize a fair number of terms. But there are tricks to memorization, and I'll show you some in the study skills workshop I'll tell you about in a couple of minutes.

Shifts position, Cut to camera B. Okay, let's talk a little about the practical side of Zoology 111. One of the first things you will notice about it is its size. There are 300 of you and one of me. This may be a bit of a shock to you, coming from high school. [My informal research suggests that this is even more shocking than I had suspected. Today's high school students are used to a close, informal relationship with their teachers. Their concern needs to be recognized, and a little reassurance is appropriate.] One of the effects of being in a big class is that you will notice that you have far more independence than you did in high school. No one will nag you about homework, but on the other hand, no one will ask you if you need help. If you get an A, you deserve all the credit. If you get an F, you deserve all the blame.

Shifts position, camera B follows. The fact that Zoo 111 is huge doesn't mean that help isn't available—it just means you have to ask for it. Before the hour is over, I'll show you just how many help resources are available to you.

Cut to camera A. Another difference you will probably notice is that I'm a lot— *meaner*—than many high school teachers. For example, I don't accept excuses. If a paper is supposed to be due Thursday at 3:00 P.M., at 3:01 P.M. I won't accept it, and you'll get a zero. Hard disc died? I don't *care.* [I try to use the tone Tommy Lee Jones used in *The Fugitive*, when Harrison Ford screamed at him that he didn't kill his wife. Jones just shrugged and said, "I don't care."] Had to go to a funeral? I don't care. Somebody stole your car with the only copy of your paper in it? I don't care. Why not? Because I give you so much time to do your assignments that you can easily turn them in a week or two early. There are *always* unforeseen circumstances, so when you do projects, you have to allow for the unexpected and start early. In this class you *cannot* wait until the last minute to study for an exam or start a project. There are many people today with nice, steady jobs flipping burgers who can tell you just how true this is. In the professions you want to go into, nobody cares about excuses. If a physician makes a mistake and kills a patient, nobody cares about what a tough day the doc had the day before. Similarly, I am unsympathetic to how many other courses you take, your part-time job work, or your family responsibilities. Why? Because I've seen students with heavier workloads and more kids than you have get As.

Shifts position. On this topic, I want to tell you about the story of the only student in the history of Zoology 111 to get 100%. Was this a brilliant kid who graduated from some exclusive prep school? No. She was a 30-year-old woman in a wheelchair [believe it or not, this is actually a true story]. She had gone directly from high school into the merchant marine. She was a sailor on a freighter. There was an accident on board, a cable snapped and cut her spinal cord in half. After rehab, she decided to go back to school so she could go into medical research on spinal cord injuries, and *nothing* was going to get in her way. And it didn't. So I *know* what students can do if they put their mind to it.

Cut to camera B. But does this explain why I'm so hard-hearted? Maybe it is just that I am a miserable specimen of a human being who enjoys bullying students and causing them misery. *Deadpan.* Actually, yes. *Grins.* No, not really, but I can explain why I'm going to be so hard on you. It is because I am not your teacher—at least not in the sense that you knew teachers in high school. [If you're going to be tough nowadays, when almost nobody has been tough on them before they came to you, unless you want to create a really hostile class atmosphere, you have to give them a fairly plausible reason why you're going to be hard-nosed. Far more students have sports experience nowadays than before, so sports metaphors are extremely valuable.] Is there anyone out there who is really good at an individual sport—track and field, skating, like that? *Points.* Yes, what's your sport? Gymnastics. Outstanding. [*Always* repeat questions or comments from the class. Acoustics in most large classrooms are one-way, so students in other parts of the auditorium generally cannot hear student comments.] Okay, let's say you were good enough to actually have some hope of making it to the Olympics. What would be the first thing you would do? Somebody said "Get an endorsement contract." Ehhhhh, wrong! That's the *second* thing you do. No, what you do first is hire the best personal trainer, the best personal coach you can afford.

Shifts position. So you find somebody who has trained a lot of winners, and you go to them and ask how much they would charge to prepare you for the Olympic try-outs. After you wake up from the shock, you talk to your parents, and if you mortgage their house, you can come up with the fee. So you go back to the coach and say, "Look, coach, I think we can manage your fee, but if we're going to spend that kind of money, we want a *guarantee* that I'll get into the Olympics."

Cut to camera A. Now, do you know what any reputable coach would say to that kind of request? "Ha, ha, ha. Surely you're joking!" *No* honest coach *can* make that kind of guarantee because there are so many things outside the coach's control—the natural ability of the athlete and his or her drive and ambition being the main things. What the good coach can promise is that the athlete will have the best possible *chance* at the Olympics under his or her direction.

Cut to camera B. So you sign up with the coach, and you start workouts. But such workouts! You've never had anything like these workouts. Why, this coach is a sadist! So finally, you can't take it anymore, and you say, "Coach, I can't take it anymore! I can't give you one more rep, let alone five. I just can't do it!"

Shifts position. Now, at this point, what do you *really* want the coach to say? Do you really want him to say, "You're right. You can't do it. Why don't you take a break now, relax a little, come back when you feel like it. After all, it's just a game, so why get in a sweat about it?" No! What you need for that coach to say is, "You can't do it? Don't give me that crap. I've trained hundreds of gymnasts, including Olympians, and you're better than most of them, so I *know* you can do it. But you're just lazy, and now you've pissed me off, so you don't owe me 5, I want 10." And you're going to be so mad at that coach that you'll give him the 10 that you're going to need to get into the Olympics.

Cut to camera A. So that's what it is. I'm not your teacher; I'm your coach, and I prepare champions. Coaches make you do things you don't want to do, like pushups or wind sprints. Coaches make you do more of these things than you would prefer to do. Coaches don't care if you're tired, or have other things to do, or think you can't do anymore. I *know* what you can do because I've prepared thousands of doctors, scientists, pharmacists, you name it. So you may think that my demands are unreasonable, but they're not, and they produce results. [Obviously, you wouldn't have to go through this if your demands were going to be modest, or if you were dealing with nonmajors. I think the biggest motivational challenge in large-class teaching is trying to run a demanding, nonmajor's course. If the subject is of inherent general interest or utility, that helps.] So this is why sleep is going to be something that you vaguely recall doing sometime in the past, you'll have to use toothpicks to keep your eyelids open, and your forefingers will develop permanent crooks from doing so much writing.

Shifts position. Now, you might be saying to yourself, "Wait a minute! I could understand this coach business if it was just you and me, but there are 300 students in this class, and there's no way that everybody here is gonna make it to the Olympics, or in this case, med school." You're right. I wish I could, but I can't say that everybody here has the potential for med school. What I *can* say is this. Somewhere in this class, I don't know exactly where, is the next Chief Wildlife Biologist for the state of Rhode Island, the next Curator of Fish for Sea World, a next Professor of Biology at Berkeley. How do I know that? Because I taught the *last* Chief, Curator, and Professor. The thing is, I don't know who that winner is. *Points.* Maybe it's you. Or you. Or you. So since I don't know who the winners are, I have to assume that you *all* are potential winners. And that is why I have to beat on you so hard as a class— it's because I have to treat you as winners, who need the kind of hard workout that champions need. When you have to start worrying is when I start treating you nice. That probably means that, as a class, you haven't shown me that you have the right stuff, and it would be cruel to make you work that hard if there's no way that you were going to make it. [It would be possible, of course, to be very demanding of the class and not go through all this rigmarole. I have found, however, that in recent years, students don't seem to understand that a demanding teacher really has their interests in mind, and this somewhat drawn-out explanation really makes a difference in class atmosphere. The students don't *like* the work, but they at least understand why the demands are being made.]

Moves over to overhead projector stand. Now, let's talk about the procedures of Zoology 111. The teaching assistants will now pass out to you a course syllabus and course instruction manual, and we'll go over the details. *TAs pass out handouts,* LECTURER *goes over details, making frequent use of the overhead.* [One might think that simply passing out a complete instruction guide would be sufficient, and it would not be necessary to go over things in class. However, some of your students may not be very good readers, and some may have what are now called learning disabilities and may get the message better through hearing, rather than reading. Plus, the title of the old Jacqueline Susann novel *Once is Not Enough* applies in spades to first-year classes. If you have really critical instructions, you need to repeat them several times, on different occasions.] *Goes through about 15 minutes of instructions.*

Dissolve away from overhead to camera A. Now let's talk about grading a little. Grading is always a kind of uncomfortable subject—I don't know *anybody* who *likes* to be evaluated. I certainly don't. But, I have to assign you a grade. [Never say "give" students a grade. That implies it is somehow a discretionary gift, an idea you want to avoid suggesting.] And I have tried hard to develop a grading system that is accurate and fair. However, I must caution you that the word "fair" often means something different in high school and university courses. In high school, "fair" usually means that if you put in a good effort and work hard in a course, you will be rewarded appropriately. In the university, it is *assumed* that you will put in a good effort and work hard—these things are *expected* and receive no special reward. What *is* rewarded is *performance*, and what "fair" now means is that if your performance is good, you should earn [again, choice of words suggesting that the grade received has more to do with the student than the professor] a good grade, and if your performance is bad, you will earn a poor grade. You already know about this in other areas; at the end of a basketball game, who wins? The team that tried the hardest, or the team with the most points? Now, I don't mean to suggest that effort and hard work aren't important—they most certainly are. But in a big class, I have no way of *knowing* whether individual people work hard or not at all. I can't measure effort or enthusiasm. And I'm sure you wouldn't want some people in this class to get good grades just because they're smooth talkers. *Whiny, wheedling voice.* "Oh, Professor Heppner, I work sooooooo hard, and I really need a B. I know I failed the first two exams, but they don't show what I really know." No, that wouldn't be fair to the students who really do work hard and have the results to show for it. So your grade is based on something I *can* measure reasonably accurately, and that is performance.

Cut to camera B. Now there are basically two systems that you can use to grade a class. *Spends the next five minutes or so explaining the grading system.* [I spend a lot of time explaining exactly why I use the grading procedures I do—why I don't use a curve, why no extra credit, why the makeup policy is what it is, etc. Students have a consuming interest in grades, so you won't lose their attention, and you can save yourself a lot of whining later on.]

Cut to camera A. There's one final aspect of grading that we need to talk about. I don't *like* to talk about it, but it has to be done. As I'm sure you know, it is the official policy of this university that cheating and its cousin plagiarism are viewed as academic crimes and treated accordingly. [This is a critical section. Nothing reduces cheating more than the attitude of the instructor. You have to make a positive and vigorous statement, in your own way, right at the beginning of the course, or you will be putting out cheating brush fires all semester. Unfortunate, but true.] Says so right in the university manual. However, as the old-timers in this class know, there are courses here where the instructor either doesn't know or doesn't care that cheating goes on, and it *is* relatively easy to cheat and get away with it. There is also a feeling in the student culture that cheating is a victimless crime—you're just cutting a little advantage for yourself, or maybe helping a friend in trouble. *Excitedly.* WRONG! WRONG! WRONG! Cheating is property theft, exactly the same both morally and practically as car theft. If you don't think it is okay to break into somebody's car and take it because yours is an old beater and breaks down all the time, then you can't believe that cheating is a victimless crime. I'll give you a demonstration of how this works.

LECTURER *moves out into the audience. Camera A zooms back and dollies with him as he moves. Camera B moves into position so it can get a close-up of his face at the appropriate time.* LECTURER *stands right next to a student on the aisle.* Okay, I'm looking for a pharmacy major. Are you a pharmacy major? Good. Now I'm going to make up a story about you, okay, I've never met you before, so this is just a story. I'm going to make up your name, too; let's call you Jason. Let's say you are a pretty good student, smart and hardworking. When you finish URI, you have a 3.1 average. Pretty good for pharmacy. Now you hear about a job opening. It is a fabulous job. Good location, good pay, lots of opportunity for advancement. And you know how tough the job market is. This is probably the best job you're ever going to get a chance at. So you apply for it. But you're not the only applicant. I need another pharmacy major. Raise hands. Okay, you. *Moves to other student.* Now again, this is a story. Your name is—Heather. Heather here is not as smart as Jason, and she certainly doesn't work as hard. If she did her own work, she'd graduate with a 2.9. But there's one thing she does very well. She cheats, and she's a real pro. She picks her courses carefully, and she's not greedy, so she's not conspicuous. Because she's so good at it, she ends up with a 3.2. Not bad, eh? But now, she hears about the job Jason applied for, and she applies for it, too. Now she and Jason have about the same courses, about the same part-time work experience, and both created a good impression in the interview. The only difference is that she has a 3.2, and Jason has a 3.1. Now, class, you're the personnel manager, and these two people are almost alike, but one has a better grade point. Which one are you going to hire? Sing it out! *The class yells, "Heather."* That's right, the cheater Heather! Now, Heather and Jason don't even know each other, but has Heather stolen anything from Jason? You're damned right she has! HEATHER HAS STOLEN THE BEST JOB JASON WOULD EVER HAVE IN HIS LIFE! HEATHER HAS STOLEN JASON'S FUTURE! And that's why cheating and plagiarism are property crimes and are treated accordingly. LECTURER *slowly walks down to position behind overhead projector.*

Cut to Camera B. As LECTURER *talks, camera very slowly zooms in on his face.* But in Zoo 111 it goes deeper than that. If you haven't been able to tell, I LOVE to teach. And my reward is the success of my good, hardworking students. I get OFF when I hear that one of my former students is doing well in medical school. Tears come to my eyes when I think about all those students who are now valuable, contributing members of society. LECTURER *becomes more agitated with each word of the following sentence.* So just the THOUGHT that some slimy little bottom-feeding MAGGOT of a scummy cheater has STOLEN the value of one of my good student's grades DRIVES ME CRAZY! *Camera is in tight on* LECTURER'S *face. He has quietly turned the lights on the electronic overhead projector upward, so his face is illuminated from below—standard movie monster lighting. He tries to convey the out-of-control, quiet-but-sinister quality of Jack Nicholson in* The Shining. So you need to know this. If you try to cheat in my class, I can't guarantee that I will catch you. No system can make that promise. LEC-TURER'S *voice gets very low, his face an unpleasant mask.* But if I DO catch you, I will not just flunk you—I will DESTROY you. I will *personally,* personally make sure that the best job you ever get in YOUR life will be cleaning toilets in a bus station. *Pauses.* And, if you think I can't do that, why—try me. *Long pause.* LECTURER *then shakes himself, almost as if recovering from a trance.* Sorry, like I said, I don't even like to talk about this, but I wanted you good, honest students, who are almost all of you, I'm sure, to know that you are going to have good protection against these parasites who would suck your blood without your even knowing they were there. [This is only one of a number of potential ways to let the class know what your position is on cheating. For example, you can express to them how disappointed you would be if they cheated, despite all your efforts to help them. Or how important it is for professionals to have a highly developed ethical sense because society puts so much trust in them. Whatever the approach, it is critical that you not make any threats you are not prepared to carry out because, in a big class, you almost surely will have your bluff, if it is a bluff, called.]

Cut to camera A. All right, let's see if I can wrap this up for you. Zoology 111 is a large class, and you have to do things a little differently in a large class than a small class to get the most out of it. All of the course procedures are in the course manual, and it is so important that we require you to sign an affidavit that you have read it. You will have to deal with two people in this course, your teaching assistant and me, and it is very important to get to know your TA, and you will have the opportunity to do so. Zoo 111 is a demanding, time-consuming course, but it has an outstanding record of turning out successful people. The subject of Zoology 111, the biology of animals, is about the most interesting subject in the world, and I'll try to share with you some of the secrets of that world that I've been fortunate enough to discover. Okay, I think that's about enough for the first day. Any questions? *Fade to black.*

The End

INDEX